My Journey to Victory

By

Onyeje Ijaola

Copyright © 2018 Onyeje Ijaola

ISBN: 978-1-60383-576-3

Published by:
Holy Fire Publishing
www.HolyFirePublishing.com

Cover Design: Jay Cookingham

Printed in the United States of America, The United Kingdom and Australia

Dedicated to

My Sweet Mother

The Late Maria Amudu (1952–1994)

Acknowledgements

Special thanks to my husband, Olusegun Ijaola, my biggest cheerleader, my greatest Supporter and loyal friend, my lover, and the father of my children. You were there through the rough times and never allowed me to give up; you believed in me and told me I had so much to give to my generation. You're such a gentle but a strong force that kept us all together. I love you more.

To our children, gifts from God, and blessings to us; life will not be the same without you guys. I love you:

Ihotu Ijaola

Joshua Ijaola

Josiah Ijaola

To my dad, Prince Gabriel Ekele Obekpa. AKA guy man, I love you.

My brothers and sisters, I appreciate and love you all; love you guys to the moon and back. AKA mega five

Nancy O. Obekpa

Ofuowoicho S. Obekpa

Ebowo R. Akin Ojo

Eneape M. Obekpa

Rose O. Obekpa

Emmanuelle E. Obekpa

Christopher E. Obekpa

Daniel Obekpa

Oguche Obekpa

A special thanks to my mother in the Lord, Mrs. Veronica Aluma, the one who led me to Jesus; you never stopped praying for me, my mentor and covering. Thank you for answering the call.

A big thanks to Moyo Akin-Ojo, and Emma Opara for your never-ending travail in prayers for me and my family.

Pastor Joseph Ogbe, you encouraged me, prayed for me and called me up even at night from Nigeria to make sure I finished this book.

Thank you, Mrs. Adebanke Kamson, for your love, prayers, and for always believing in me.

To my Pastors Joseph and Misti Coyne, it is an honor doing life with you.

To all my friends and those whom I didn't mention, I love and appreciate you all.

Rise up from the ashes and put on beauty. Clothe yourself with the garment of praise. Exchange sorrow for the oil of joy... Rise up in power and walk in the fullness of who God has created you to be.

Isaiah 61:3

You are worth it.

CONTENTS

PART I: MY STORY

Chapter 1: My Parents

It's the time of the year when the trees begin to change color, the weather changes and begins to cool off, and the soft breeze of fall arrives, that I look from my window and wonder how something that is dying can look so beautiful. As I stood and pondered, I drifted back to 1975, the year I was born to two wonderful parents, Prince Gabriel Obekpa and Maria Amadu.

I was born in the beautiful city of Jos, the capital of Plateau state. The landscape was of Rocky Mountains made up of granite rocks with beautiful sceneries; the climate was perfect—it was semi-temperate with temperatures only ranging between 64 Fahrenheit and 25. The Plateau state is home to the ancient Nok culture, known for its remarkable terracotta art work. It was culturally diverse, and the people spoke Berom and Angas. Plateau state was a good tourist attraction before the tribal conflicts between Christians and Muslims.

My Mother Maria was born in 1952 in Benue state, Nigeria. When she was fifteen years old, the civil war started. The civil war, also known as the Biafran war, went from July 6, 1967 until January 15, 1970; the war lasted for 3 years in the southeastern part of Nigeria; it was a war fought between the government of Nigeria and the secessionist state of Biafra. Biafra represented the nationalist aspirations of the Igbo people, whose leadership felt they could no longer coexist with the Northern-dominated Federal government. The conflict resulted from political, economic, ethnic, cultural and religious tensions which preceded Britain's formal decolonization of Nigeria from 1960 to 1963. Immediate causes of the war in 1966 included a military coup, a counter-coup and persecution of Igbos living in Northern Nigeria. Control over the lucrative oil production in the Niger Delta played a vital strategic role. Within a year, the Federal Military Government surrounded Biafra, capturing coastal oil facilities and the city of Port Harcourt. The blockade imposed during the ensuing stalemate led to severe famine. During the two and a half years of the war, there were about 100,000 overall military casualties, while between 500,000 and 2 million Biafran civilians died from starvation.

As the war waxed stronger, my mother, then 15 years old, had to flee with her parents to a safer place and migrated to Jos and settled in that region. In the era when my mother was born, education was not open to girls as they were more of domestic help and married off early to start their own families; my mother was the first among five siblings, and at the time was not allowed to go to school.

In the fifties, Nigeria was still under British colonial rule, so missionaries came from Europe to build schools and hospitals in the region. A missionary had spotted my mother and came to her parents' home one day to talk to them about allowing my mother to go to school. My mother began her elementary school and went on to start

10

secondary school. She had to leave Jos to go to an all-girls boarding school in Kabba (Okaba) in the mid-west part of Nigeria. In school they learned basic math, English and health science. My mother was an excellent student and in no time became a favorite of the teachers and landed on the principal's Honor list. She was good in math and science but had an artistic side to her also; she drew all the time. She told me while she was in school as a teenager she had sketched her principal and placed the picture on the wall; everyone passed by to look at the portrait she had drawn, she did so good a job, but she thought she was going to get in trouble for sketching her principal. When the principal found out about the portrait, she was called and awarded for the excellent job.

After five years, all the girls had completed their education and had plans to go back home and continue life without the slightest idea of what the future had in store for them, but my mother among so many was selected to go to England where she would continue her education in Queens College, London. It was a prestigious all-girls school. My mother was so happy as she ran home to tell her parents. Her parents were skeptical and did not understand what was going to happen to their daughter. The missionaries had to visit my grandparents at the time to convince them that she was going to be well taken care of, and after her education she would safely return home.

My grandparents arranged for my mother to choose a suitor and get married before she moved to England. My mother told me she had to decide between my dad and so many other suitors that came to ask for her hand in marriage. As she told me the story, I could see in the corner of her eyes she had loved my dad with a deep love. She described my dad as tall and handsome, strong, and had fought in the Congo war. My mother had told my dad that the only way she would agree to marry him was for him to retire from the military and get a regular job. She said it was not an easy decision for him, but he did and they both got married in a very quiet ceremony in her parents' home.

My father rarely told us stories about his father; he was the third child of his mother, who was one of his father's wives but could not remember what number she was in ranking; his father was a polygamist which was a customary practice at the time. The more resources you had, the more wives and children, servants and housekeepers who helped in the farms and domestic work. My grandfather, Chief Obekpa Ejema, was the ruler of the Idoma people and was revered among the people. The stories around my grandfather were very mysterious, and all we knew about him was that he had many wives and so many children, he was rich and rode on horses, he wrapped his head in a turban, and when he came out of his palace the women were not allowed to see him; they said he was generous and ruled the people fairly. My grandfather passed away in 1960 when the civil war had started, so I never got to meet him. My dad was only 13 years old when his father passed, and his mother passed in 1971, when he was 24 years old. My dad told us very little about his childhood;

he always repeated stories about the civil war and the Congo war. He was very proud of his military accomplishments. He showed us black and white pictures of himself in his military uniform, decorated with bullets. He was very fascinated with war generals; he would watch war movies on Sarturday mornings until afternoon before going to his community meetings. My father was a very content man and had so many life lessons to teach us. I remember growing up as a teenager, my dad would sit in the living room and watch General Paton for four hours straight with my younger brother, Ofu; they'd watched "The Longest Day," and a few of his favorite American war movies by Robert Aldrich, "The Dirty Dozen." It was funny how they watched the same movies repeatedly in black and white and never got tired. Those TV screens were not any bigger than a small box.

My dad enjoyed a lot of music and he had a lot of collections. We had old Christmas songs on those records, like Boney M, ABBA, Village People, West African Beats, High-Life music with King Sunny Ade (Juju music) and Fela. My dad is a good dancer and he would dance with my mom while we watched.

Although I never met my grandparents from my father's side, he showed us very old rusty pictures of them in black and white. Those pictures looked so faded we could hardly make out any images. My dad didn't know exactly how old his parents were. In those days, people looked at the seasons to tell when they were born. My father had moved with his brother to Lagos as a teenager when his dad had died, and he did not come back home to the village until he was much

13

older. He remained with his older brother until he was old enough to join the army. He joined the Nigerian army and served in the army until he was twenty-two years old and married my mother when she was eighteen. When my dad left the military, he got a job with a supermarket in Jos called Chanria; he worked as a store clerk and later became the manager. Most of those years were quite vague in my memories.

Chapter 2: My Birth

My mother lived in England for four years; she was coming home whenever she could. While she was abroad studying, she became pregnant with her first child and came home to have her baby, who later died. He was stillborn, as I was told. My mother was about eight months pregnant when she was bitten by a vicious dog on her way back one night from a neighbor's house. Even though she had multiple rabies shots with the pregnancy, that caused her to lose her baby; it was a very hard time for my parents. The following year she got pregnant again and had my older sister Nancy. My mother, after weaning her baby, left Nancy with her mother, my grandmother; she went back to England to complete her education.

Four years after the birth of my sister, my mother became pregnant again and had me. I was a happy, chubby baby, a 9-pounder at birth. I was so big that everyone who carried me pulled on my cheek.

My father wanted me to stay with my grandmother because I was so tender, and he could not take care of me alone. My father had to work in the store and could not care for me by himself. My father later travelled to England to visit my mother, and this was my early childhood until my mother finally came back from England.

I remember growing up in my grandmother's house until I was the age of five. I would go with my grandmother to the market where she sold grains, and I would sit with her under the shed in the open market.

Watching the people pass by and the children playing in the sand and muddy water, my grandmother always kept me close by her side. When the day was over we would go back home. With the money my grandmother made from selling grains, she would purchase vegetables and yams and carry them on her head while we walked home; I didn't see a car or remember seeing one. Most people walked or rode bicycles.

My grandmother always made me hot Bonvita and gave me a huge chunk of Bread that was never sliced and a glub of Blue band margarine. My grandmother would bathe me and put me in her bed at night; she would walk me to the latrine outside to wee. She would carry a little lantern, to see in the dark of the night. I was always afraid of going outside at night. There was no electricity back then in the 70's. Houses had latrines built outside the main house; it was scary— night was very deep. If darkness could speak, you would hear all kinds of animal sounds in the dead of the night. We used lanterns and kerosene lamps to find our path.

In 1977, six years after the civil war was over, my parents decided to go back to the state they had originally come from. Benue state used to be Benue Plateau before it was divided into two. My parents moved to Benue state. We traveled at the time in a train to our new state, and my father moved my grandparents, his in-laws, along with the whole family; he took them back to their village, Otukpa, and we settled in Makurdi, about two-and-a-half hours away.

My mother got a job working as a nurse/midwife and later matron of the general hospital in Makurdi, which was the capital of our new State. She also worked as a nursing instructor at the school of nursing at the time. We lived in the housing estate provided for us by the Govenment.

My father had resigned from his supermarket manager job to seek new opportunities in Benue; the jobs were hard to find, and most people who lived in Benue State at that time were farmers. The land was very fertile, and it was called The Food Basket of the Nation. Gradually my father, being the entrepreneur that he is, could not sit and wait for handouts; he was determined to make it in life and provide for his family. He had no car, but he had a bicycle, and with the bicycle he would ride around picking up empty Coca-Cola bottles for recycling and reselling them back to the company. In those days, you could not buy Coke or Fanta without a bottle exchange. Over time, he made enough money to buy a motorcycle, but he did not stop collecting recyclable bottles until he had a little space in the corner of our room stacked up with empty Coca-Cola crates. My dad saved enough money, and with the help of my mother, he bought a little white Peugeot pickup truck. I can still remember how excited we were; we had a car; that was a major step up for us at the time. Before long my dad was selling Coca-Cola crates and became a distributor for the company. With the money he made he started laying a foundation for our first house, but then decided to turn it into a mini-inn where people could lodge and rent rooms.

In 1978, my brother Ofuowoicho, which means God's Power, was born. We all just called him Ofu. My dad was so desperate for a male child and had waited so long for this child, that Ofu was welcomed with much merry-making and pomp. My father at the time felt a great sense of accomplishment for an heir was born, a male child that would carry his family name. My brother came out of the womb very dark-skinned; he was so dark that at night or when it was dark, you could see only the whiteness of his eyes. A maid was hired to take care of Ofu. He was treated like something had dropped out of heaven; when he cried, my father was on his feet. My brother was so spoiled that I made it a point of duty to pick on him at every and any opportunity. Even as a child, Ofu got irritated easily and hated for anyone to touch him or touch his lips. He was afraid of dirt; if he lived in America he would have been labeled a germaphobic. He cried when he woke up from sleep, when he was hungry, when his food was too hot, if he didn't have his way, and even if he had his way. One incident I'll never forget: Ofu's maid had sliced some fresh oranges and the orange skin was not taken off properly; the orange was not ripe enough, so when Ofu ate the oranges, he immediately developed an allergic reaction—his lips were swollen, and the more he cried, the bigger his lips grew; the help was so scared, we all thought she was going to meet her maker that day. My father was not home at the time it happened, but when he got home, he saw what had happened and was not pleased. The help made all the apologies and begged for forgiveness, but she was sent away from our house forever, and we never saw her again.

18

My father was upset with everyone for days; after about a day, Ofu's lips were back to normal. Just because he cried all the time, his eyes were always red, so we nicknamed him "Red the Wino." My brother and I fought all the time; I knew if I picked on him, at least I'd get my father's attention.

It was time for me to start elementary school, and I was enrolled in the same public school as my older sister—St. Catherine's Primary School. Across from the public school was a Catholic private school, adjacent to the public school's football field. It had a little fence around it, and I was very curious and wanted to know what went on at that school. I would leave my public school and walk over and put my face on the barbed wires around the convent. I did this everyday for about a week, then one day I saw the most amazing thing. The school was run by Catholic nuns who had sworn to a life of celibacy and purity, whatever that meant at the time; they had long blue gowns with white trimmings around their veils, and long rosary beads around their necks; they marched around the building and went to a chapel and knelt down for hours reciting their rosaries and making signs across their faces and chest. At the time I didn't know what that meant, but not long afterward, I found out it was the sign of the cross, a religious act to signify and identify with the cross by the Catholics. My family did not go to church, and we did not talk about those things at home. I continued this pattern for days and weeks non-stop, then one day after school, I told my dad I wanted to go to that school across from our house, close by the public school. My dad was not convinced, but I told him I would not go back to the public school unless I went to the school across from our house.

A week after this conversation with my dad, I was still attending the public school, and as my common practice was, I was leaning on the wires. I heard a sweet gentle voice behind me saying, "Hello, little lady; are you lost?" As I turned around, I saw an almost pale-looking woman with a long nose and blue eyes looking down at me. As she bent over to talk to the little 4-year-old, she said, "My name is Sister Alley, one of the sisters of the Nativity; what is your name?"

I said, "Onyeje" with a huge smile that stretched across one ear to the other, with 4 missing teeth.

She said, "Come with me." I was not afraid. I followed the nun to the convent, I made myself comfortable, I told her I wanted to go to her school, and I wanted her to come talk to my papa. She said, "This is a Catholic private school," and she would see how she could help me.

I was so excited I got up and gave her a huge hug. She got up and went into a kitchen and brought back a slice of cake and something to drink. I threw caution to the wind and ate the cake and drank the punch. Growing up, we had rules in our home—we never accepted food from strangers and we never ate outside of our home. I did eat the cake; it was good, too. I told Sister Alley, "Thank you," and had to go home before my dad found out I had not gone to school.

As she escorted me out, my father was at the gate of the convent looking for me. When I raised up my eyes, I was so scared I thought that was going to be my last day on earth! My eyes were so big I could not close them; if you have African parents, you can identify with this secnerio; I had left school and eaten in a stranger's house. I didn't know what to say. I had cake crumbs all over my mouth, and it was too late to wipe them off. My father was courteous to the nun and told her not to worry about me enrolling in the private school, because he could not afford for all of his children at the time to attend the school. Sister Alley said she understood.

As she closed the doors behind her, I felt something on my head that made me forget for a moment what my name was. I heard birds chirp in my ears—my father had just given me his famous Knock. I could not cry; in my little mind all I could do was breathe—no conversations whatsoever; it was a quiet night.

My father was a man of few words but did what he said he would do. A few months came by and my father enrolled me in Nativity Private School, and I started my elementary school all over again. It was a very happy time for me in primary school. I looked forward to going to school. We did not live far from school, and I could walk to school every morning. I started kindergarten, and from all I could remember, we did not do much at school. We had daily assembly where we stood in straight lines and sang the National Anthem and the Pledge and a prayer before the principal. Our class teachers went through the line and asked us to stick our fingers out for inspection; our nails were checked to make sure they were short and clean; we were not allowed to plait or grow out our hair, so there was not much difference with the boys; we all had low-cut tops and dresses; the boys had shorts and well-tucked-in shirts. Our school uniform was a red-checked shirt and navy-blue pinafore, with knee-length white socks and brown leather sandals. My dad always bought us Clark's sandals.

After the assembly ended with the school prinicpal's announcements for the day, we marched to our different classrooms in a straight line from kindergarten to primary five. When we sat in class, we waited for our teacher to come into the classroom, after she took a little time to chit-chat with her teacher friends; as she walked back into class she had the most serious look. As our teacher walked in, the class monitor knocked on the wooden locker and yelled "Class, rise," in a sing-song tune, then we all stood to our feet. The second knock goes off and we all in unison said, "Good morning, teacher."

"Good morning, friends," she would acknowledge, and had us sit down. She handed out papers, pencils, and crayons for the day. It was forbidden for us to talk in class; we paid attention and looked forward to our break times. We sang Nursery Rhymes ("London Bridge is Falling Down," "Old Roger is dead," "Tomma is a Boy," and so on). We started learning the Alphabet and how to pronounce and read words. We had our long break at 10:.30–11:30. We ate whatever lunch we brought from home, and mine was always nabisco biscuits and Caprisun juice. I always ate lunch on my way to school in the morning and played in the sand at break time until it was time to go back to class. We had our short break (bathroom breaks) at 12:45 until 1:00 p.m. and came back to class for homework. School was over at 2 p.m. I went home everyday and didn't do much in my kindergarten to second grade.

But as I started the 3rd grade (primary 3) through 4th grade (primary 4), school started to take a different turn with more serious academic work, even though it was a school run by Catholic nuns; some of the teachers were regular folks, and my favorite teacher at the time in elementary school was Mr. Jacobs. He was the best storyteller and made up stories from scratch. Most of the students in Nativity loved Mr. Jacobs. He had his little switch to dicipline and had a lot of bogus tales to go along with it; no one questioned Mr. Jacobs. He kept us engaged, and we sang the same songs over and over every day.

Even as an adult so many years later, I can remember a lot of my nursery rhymes. I remember one song about the flowers that grew in an English country garden, how many gentle flowers grow in an old English garden; how about the thousand times we sang, "Jack be nimble, Jack be quick, Jack jump over the candlestick," or songs about "I am a little tea pot" and "Old king Cole was a merry old soul."

My best time of class was our library day when we didn't have to sit on those hard stools all day, but we walked in a straight line to the library across from the headmistress's office; the principal or headmistress at the time was Rev. Sister Ann. I loved looking at all the books, and we were allowed to read for one hour; I remember reading my first library book, *Alice in Wonderland*, and more books I discovered in the same library were books like *Beauty and the Beast*, *Aladdin*, and *Cinderella*, so on and so forth. It broadened my imagination, and I didn't know if I quite understood at the time how to place the image of where all the stories were taking place; as a kid, everything was reality. It was a different world when I entered into those books; my inquisitive mind was determined to find out if this was for real; it was very different from the type of books I had been reading in class literature; very different from books like *Eze Goes to School* (by Onuora Nzekwu), *Chike and the River* (Chinua Achebe), *The First Corn* by Mbel Segun, *How the Leopard Got His Claws*, and the famous *Agbo Malaika*, *Ali* and *Simbi*, and the list goes on.

My quest for knowledge and the desire to learn became so great, I read more books and borrowed books from the library to read at home and day-dreamed of this land that I would one day live in—the land where people had transparent skin and hair long to the floor. I talked about it to my friends when we played, and they laughed very hard at me and called me crazy.

Not too long afterwards, things started changing in our home as my father started increasing in his small business; he made enough money to build his first house about fifteen minutes' drive from school, and we had to move to our new home. We were excited about the move, knowing that we had moved up in stature—we now owned our own home and we had a family vehicle. I said goodbye to our neigbors and friends I had made over the years when we moved back from Jos; now we had the pleasure of been dropped off at school and picked up; no more walking to school.

By the year 1982, Ofu had joined me in Nativity, and that was the same year my sister Ebowo was born. Her name means: "We asked God." Our family was growing, and it was the perfect time for us to have moved to our own home. Ebowo brought a lot of Joy to my parents, as my dad said that she reminded him of his mother; she was a beautiful child and the fourth born of my parents; we were a happy bunch, and we all waited on Ebowo and took turns caring for her, and as was the norm in our household, a maid was hired to care for her also. Ebowo grew up fast because she had older siblings. She was very smart and always knew what she wanted. I took it upon myself to pick on her like I did Ofu. Ebowo always wanted to do the right thing and did not like to stir up trouble; right from the cradle she knew what she wanted, if that was the right thing to say. She didn't like onions and would not touch her vegetables; I always stood close to her at mealtime and made sure I took whatever she didn't eat, which was almost half her portion.

When she turned three years old, she joined us in Nativity and started pre-kindergarteen. Right from the very beginning she was an excellent student and did very well in school, smart as a wit and was never intimidated.

Eneape joined the gang in 1983. Her name means "Mother of all." She would be my mother's last born, a very happy and contented baby. She was very calm from the womb. She came in at birth full of life and loved to drink tea. I became the tea-maker. She was everyone's sweetheart, a gentle soul and very laid back. She was the go-to person and the peacemaker as we later found out in our adult life. Before long she had joined us in the same primary school. We were now four in total at Nativity Private School and were getting really popular with the school administrators.

Not long after, I started experiencing bullying in school; I was born with a protruding umbilical hernia, and it stood out very ugly when I wore a dress. The kids around me started to notice that I had a funny shape every time I had my uniform on, and it got worse when the school changed the pinafore to a sky-blue gown for girls. The band on the waistline of my pinafore that held my protruding umbilical cord was gone, and I could not hide it anymore. The kids would come close to me and pinch my belly and run off laughing, leaving me crying. This continued and got worse until I could no longer take it. I had to tell my father what was going on. At the time this was not considered bullying; the school authorities didn't get involved with matters like this; my dad told me to stand up for myself and fight back, and I did.

By this time I had made two friends, Tina and Julie, who always told me it was okay to have a huge belly button; they played with me and kept the other kids from messing with me. We are all grown women now and still keeping in contact but live in different countries. Julie was my neighbor; she lived directly opposite from our house, and their father owned a printing press adjacent to our house. During the holidays we'd go in there and help stack papers and clean up for fun, and Julie's dad would always give us a couple of naira for helping.

Chapter 3: First Year in Boarding School

By the time I was ten years old it was time most girls and boys started preparing for secondary school in sixth grade. We wrote common entrance exams and chose schools that best fit our family and financial capabilities. I sat for the entrance exams and was picked to go to St. Ann's Secondary School in Otukpo, which was about one hour away from Makurdi. I had been going to a Catholic school, and this was the beginning of new chapter in my life. Going to a junior secondary school (JSS) was a big step for anyone and for most families. Most people went to boarding schools; it was a great accomplishment. My older sister Nancy at the time had already started her secondary school and was going to form three, JSS 3 at Fatima Girls' College in Okpoga. She was going to move to this new school with me because my parents felt it would be a clever idea to help me adjust in boarding school and bring my sister a little closer to Makurdi.

My older sister Nancy is an amazing big sister; she always assumed the role of a mother and was physically and emotionally stronger than anyone ever gave her credit for. I remember one time at our old house, my mom had just finished marking her students' papers from the nursing school, and my father was getting ready to listen to the evening news when we heard a loud knock on the door; as the door open, it was a mother and her son. The boy's mother was frantic and screaming at the top of her lungs while holding a bloody bandage on her son's head. At first my mother thought the boy had just fallen and broken his skull and needed help; she jumped to her feet and rushed to the boy, but no, that was not the case; the boy had come with his mom to accuse Nancy of breaking his head while at school, and he came to identify who had done it. My sister was in the middle of the living room at the time, and when she was questioned about what happened, she said in a very nonchalant attitude, "The boy was messing with me, and I picked up a stone and broke his head, so he could leave me alone." Silence, total shock, and much disbelief filled the room, but guess who giggled. My mother calmed the boy's mom, took the boy to the bathroom, washed his head, and provided first aid; the boy's head was not broken. My mom asked the mother to bring him to the general hospital in the morning if he became worse and the bleeding did not stop. We had no emergency room services at the time and still do not have one. When they left, my mom and dad talked to Nancy, but silently I guess my dad was happy that she stood up for herself at school.

My sister and I ended up in the same secondary school, located in Otukpo. I was in JSS 1 and she was in JSS 3. The journey was an hour-long drive, sitting in the back of my father's Peugeot 504, and the lectures continued. My father spoke for almost forty-five minutes on how I should conduct myself in this new school, and not bring disgrace to the family; "Study your books and make sure you pass and come first in class." All our parents wanted every child to come first in class; if they had seven children in one class, they wanted all seven to come first in class, and all African parents, including mine, all came first in class. In modern interpretation, you must have all A+ to be ahead of everyone in your class. My father dropped us off, gave us our pocket money and provisions, and drove off. I had a brand-new mattress, a cutlass, a metal bucket, a set of cutleries, two metal bowls, a box full of provisions, powdered milk, Bonvita, the famous cabin Biscuit, St. Louis sugar, a giant tube of Vaseline and Nivea cream, combs, Mosquito net, Ijebu gari cereal, and the list goes on.

This was my first day at St. Ann's Secondary School in Otukpo at the age of nine; I'd be almost 10 years old in a few months. The girls who arrived before me came up to help me, and they carried my bags to my dormitory; I didn't know anyone, except for my older sister. I was put in the same dormitory with her. The senior students had to sleep on the lower bunks, and the junior students had to sleep on the top bunks. My domitory was named Cornelia and had thirty bunk beds— fifteen bunk beds in one row, making two rows in the rectangular room. The beds were turned so our legs faced inward and our heads turned far on the opposite side to keep us quiet after lights out. In between the bunk beds was a narrow walkway with built-in shelves where we could mount our metal boxes made by the metalsmith man. We didn't carry luxury boxes to school; we had huge padlocks on our boxes, and the key was always strapped around our wrists or around our necks as pendants. We had little corners on the side of our beds where we had wooden lockers about 24 inches in height and 24 inches wide; we stored our provisions in the bedside lockers. There were 30 girls in that dormitory ranging from age nine to eighteen. I stored the rest of my belongings that could not fit into the tiny wooden locker underneath my bed. My bucket, bathing sponge, and rubber bathroom slippers—everything that was mine—was marked with huge initials even up to my underwear.

It was a very different environment, and my first day ever being away from home. I knew from the very moment I walked in there that I wasn't going to make it through. The environment felt like a military camp or prison. There were gates around the school; we could not leave the school premises; it was like a convent. While these thoughts were going through my mind, the bell began to ring, and I saw all the girls running with their soup bowls and cutlery, all dressed in green and white-checked bubas and wrappers. Up until then, I had never tied on a wrapper; I quickly opened my box, changed as fast as I could into my compound uniform as it was called; my wrapper was half-tied and dragging along as I ran with my soup bowl and cutlery toward the direction all the girls were running to. We all stood in line, and for a nine-year-old, I was tall, so I could see what was going on in front of me. It was dinner time at 6 p.m.; we filed into the dining area and sat at wooden tables and waited for our turn to get food. We all began to talk to one another; right then I spotted a girl called Ori who had attended the same elementary school. I called her name out with a loud voice and waved at her, and immediately we started talking and giggling until a nun walked in to silence everyone and to say grace before the meal. We repeated the same prayer for each meal from then on.

My table was called and as I walked closer to the food window, I saw steaming hot, giant pots that could fit four people inside, and a huge charcoal fire and huge cooking spoons and ladles. The women in that kitchen were huge, tall, strong women that worked over the years in that extreme condition. Their skin looked rubbery and their hands looked all shriveled up from years of cooking for over five hundred students. The only emotions you saw out of these women was a smile; they handled those hot pots with their bare hands and did not say a word. As I looked in amazement, I heard a loud and firm voice say, "Bring your plate." She dumped a spoon of some sort of slimy soup into my plate and a piece of dried, cooked yam. As I went back to my table, I sat down and huge tears rolled down my cheeks. I was so afraid and thought I was going to starve, and no one would help me; I could not eat the food. From that day, I silently started planning my escape from that school!

After dinner was over at 6:30, the huge bells rang again, and we filed out to our classroom for night prep study until 7:30. The generators were left on for reading and homework. At 7:45 p.m., we all had to go back to our dormitories and make our beds. The bell rang again at 8:30, and that was lights out. We all went to bed.

My day started at 5.30 a.m. when the bells rang. I don't care how deep your sleep was, those bells could wake a dead person. We had to go to the bathrooms built outside and detached; from the dormitories, which were cold and dark, we could hear the animals and crickets and all kinds of night sounds, even though it was in the morning, but it was so dark. The roosters crow at dawn, and we all took our little metal buckets that could hold about three gallons of water to the well to fetch our bathing water. I quickly learned it was better to fetch the water in the evening and hide it under my bed for use the next day. First thing in the morning, I wouldn't have to join the long lines at the well, and at least have a little dry spot to bathe. The only disadvantage of getting the water a day before was the water was cold in the morning; I was used to waking up in the morning with boiling water mixed to lukewarm water for my baths, but not anymore. We had no way of heating our bath water in boarding school; all electric gadgets were contraband. You could get suspended if caught with any electrical appliance. We had charcoal pressing irons that worked well but needed skill to use. I never ironed my uniforms; at nine years old, I could hardly match up the right uniform, let alone iron one. So when I got my water from the well, it took about 3 draws to fill my bucket up; the bathroom was nasty mud with water everywhere, so I just stood outside and poured water on my face and ran back inside. I was caught doing that one day and spent half my day weeding grass as punishment for taking my bath outside.

At 6 a.m., we pulled out our holy rosaries, and uniforms of white blouses and black skirts, with white scarf, and walked 2 miles to St. Frances Catholic Church for morning Mass. It was at an all-boys

Catholic school. I lagged behind the line and cried all the way through the walk there. If I could not find my knee-high, white socks and was halfway dressed. I knew I was going to get spanked or punished for not wearing the proper uniform to class. While at Mass, I could hardly concentrate; all I thought about was going back home. I was homesick; I missed my mother, and I missed the comfort of my home. A few weeks prior to boarding school, I was being bathed and waited upon, I could eat what I wanted, sleep and play in the sand, and watch TV. But now I had to grow up in this camp called boarding school. I was miserable; half the time my hair was not even combed.

I hated going to morning Mass; it was boring, and everyone sang in Latin and read in Latin. I'll bet half of what they sang was made up. How did some bunch of Idoma folks learn to sing in Latin? It was funny how some of the people wanted to outshine the others by singing off key. I was a junior student and was not going to get a slap after Mass, so I controlled myself and held my tongue, but I was between the words shut up or let out a loud laugh, which was my way of responding to an uncomfortable situation. I didn't understand what I was saying half the time in Latin, but we all faked the serious look and kept our hands in the pious prayerful position like that of Mary the mother of Jesus in the pictures. I needed a halo around my head to complete my outfit. We just repeated stuff and made the sign of the cross for everything and for nothing. The priest walked around the altar with the incense, and in no time we all smelled like myrrh.

As the priest walks around the altar two or three times, he stops and faces the parishioners, waves the sign of the cross, and in a loud, sing-song, fake-Italian accent, that sounds more like an Idoma man from my village, he says, "Nomine Patris et filii et Spiritus Sancti," and everybody responds in a singing voice: "Aaaaaammeeeeeenn."

As Mass was over, out we went again in a file in the cold and 2-mile walk back to school and straight to breakfast; we had millet porridge and bean cakes, Akara, etc.

After a few weeks, staying in school became more difficult; I was not adjusting well. I could not handle my situation any longer. At this point, half of what I brought with me was stolen or missing, my older sister had missed too many classes trying to take care of me, and my teachers about had it. All I heard was, "This child is not ready for school and may be a little spoiled."

I went to the principal's office and demanded to go back home; she looked at me straight in the face and said, "Ms. Obekpa, you need to go back to class before I call your father. You have visiting days once a month on the second Sarturday of every month for three hours. If you need some money you can have some reserve your father left for you and your sister from the House mistress, but I am sorry I cannot let you go home." I stormed out of her office back to class.

Ori my friend came over to talk to me and tried to calm me down; she seemed to be doing better than me in adjusting, so that day we both planned on how we could make this school a better place for all the girls our age, and that's how the planning began.

At prep time, Ori and I did not study; we went around from one class to the next making jokes and pranks. We got a lot of attention doing that and got noticed by the senior students; they would pull Ori and I out and make us clown, dance, and just entertain them, and at the end of the evening we had an extra cabin biscuit and dry milk. It wasn't so bad after all. I was learning to survive a little, then I took it to the next level. I would laugh during Mass because I thought the priest was funny, then I would get in trouble and drag other girls along with me. By the end of my second week, I was popular. More of the girls gave me their food and wanted to make friends with me because I was breaking the rules and getting away with it.

I didn't take school work seriously; I played all the time. I didn't wash my uniforms, I didn't do the portion of my day chores, and my home work was not done. One morning Ori and I had stayed up all night talking from across our bunk beds and were sneaking out to go eat food from our lockers, since we stayed hungry all the time. A senior caught us, and we got in big trouble; the next day we skipped Mass, and spent the first part of school washing toilets for punishment. We had so much fun doing it because I for one did not want to go to Mass or class; I was enjoying my new-found freedom. I giggled in class and made funny faces when my teachers were teaching and made the whole class laugh until I got pulled out, and for the rest of the class I was on my knees with my eyes closed and my hands above my head.

36

By this time, I had survived a few weeks, and on my first visiting day, my father could not come because he was on a business trip, and my mother did not come either because she had other commitments. Ori's parents came, so I tagged along with her for the remainder of the day. Visiting day was such a joyful time, we all woke up early, and wore our day dresses and waited for our names to be called, so we could join our parents in the hall. Most girls never had anyone visit them, but my dad could come to my school anytime he wanted, and I would get pulled out of class to the principal's office to go visit with him.

On a Wednesday afternoon my dad came to visit me, and I was called to go out and meet him. I went with a bunch of my friends to greet him; he was smiling and knew that I had a lot to say. After greeting him in my language, I said "Papa, I want to come home; I don't want to stay here anymore; I'm suffering," and the list went on.

He laughed and said, "This will build you up and you will grow up to be strong." He gave me more provisions and money, and my sister was with me as well with a few of her friends; he instructed her to take care of me and to keep me in line. My father was a very generous man; he gave all my friends that came with me money, and as was the custom for young girls at the time, they knelt and thanked him. Now I knew for sure if I had to leave this school, Ori and I had to come up with another plan.

It was the end of the first term, our final exams were done, and it was time to go home for a long vacation—what we call here in America a summer holiday. We were a total of 40 girls in one class, and we had to rank from the 1st position to the 40th. We took pride in education and whoever came first in class was like a hero, and everyone looked up to them. The difference between 1st and 2nd could be one point. So we got our grades, our bags were packed, and we all stayed close to the gates waiting to get picked up by our parents or drivers. Parents came and the school started to empty out. Then came our car with the driver; he came to a screeching halt. He was a short guy with a bad temper, and he didn't like me in particular because I made fun of him a lot. My sister and I watched him pack our stuff into the car and then we hopped into the car. He drove us an hour and a half back to Makurdi. I was so happy to see home, my mother, and my room after three months. My mother made me shower immediately; she washed my hair and gave me clean clothes to wear.

Then it was time to prove my three months of school. My father wanted to see my report card. My sister did very well as always, and then I saw my dad's eye get bigger and bigger as he moved toward me. I kept taking a few steps toward the door. I knew that look; it was the "run for your life" look; before I could, my father had grabbed me by my arm and asked me in English mixed with Idoma and some few choice words: "What is this type of report card? … Is this what I sent you to boarding school for? …What are you thinking? Bloody fool, are you crazy?"

And I kept saying, "No sir, yes sir." And then for a moment I realized I didn't even know what report card I had; I didn't even know my

38

grades because we were not even allowed to open the envelope until we gave it to our parenets. Well I came in 39th out of 40, and I mustered the courage to say at least I didn't come in 40th, or at least someone else had the worst grade. And at that moment my dad almost threw me across the room, but he didn't. That was not the time to giggle, because I could feel it coming up on the inside of me; my teachers note was: "Onyeje is a motor girl; she plays too much and sleeps in class." Somehow, I felt I had achieved the right to now stay back at home from going to that boarding school.

My dad was upset for 2 days, but before you knew it, home was normal again and I had a long sweet vacation. In those days telephones were not so popular and a luxury in so many homes, like TVs and so on. I could not call or communicate with a bunch of my friends, but I played with our neigbours who lived across from us. Julie and I played together with Martina during the holidays, but we all went to different boarding schools, so we all had made new friends but visited and played together during the holidays and talked about our experinces. Our neighbours were devout Catholics, so they went to Masses all the time, morning and evening. My parents did not go to church and pretty much did not do many religious activities, but as we started growing older, St. Theresa was a Catholic church that was a walk away from our home, so on Sunday mornings my parents would give us money and make us go to church. My brother Ofu and my three sisters would go to the Catholic church and sit through the songs in the children's church under a tree. How can I ever get over those songs in children's church? I hear them playing in my head right now. Then we'd run out and play in the heap of white construction sand, and when Mass was over we used our money to buy Allewa, a traditional-made hard candy on a stick, and Donkuwa. We looked forward to Sundays and we did that for many years and even had catechism classes where we learnt Latin and Roman Catholic History.

At this point, my dad would come to the Bazaars more like a fund-raiser once every year, and sometimes would be made the chairman of the occasion. And as children and teenagers, it was an opportunity to hang out and meet people; it was like a carnival. It was the time of the year the Catholic Church raised morney by selling food items and through auctioning things brought into the house by offerings; it was also an opportunity for priests to drink beer from a plastic cup. I am not sure if the beer was a sin since they had real wine at Communion; anyway, every year we moved around from one bazaar to another from St. Theresa to Holy Ghost in Wadata and to the big Cathedral where the popular people and rich Catholics hung out. Those bazaars were hiding grounds for girls who had boyfriends and didn't want their parents to find out; they met there, and all kinds of things happened at those bazaars.

After the summer was over, it was time to go back to school. I did not want to go back to school and I didn't know how best to tell my mom and dad. As the normal practice in our home, we had to write a list of provisions and go to the tailors to get measured for new school uniforms, then to the barbers to get our hair cut before going back to school; that was the most difficult part, we all longed to have that beautiful, long, silky hair we saw on TV, and I always fantasized about growing my hair all the way to my waist, and after I read the story of Rapunzel, I always wondered how painful it was to have your hair for a ladder. We talked about Rapunzel's hair in our little girl time talk, and hair was a huge deal since we were not allowed to grow ours; it was seen as a distraction, drawing too much attention to the girls in school. It was said that girls who braided their hair spent too much time on how they looked and never spent enough time reading. Most schools in Nigeria at the time did not allow girls to braid their hair. My siblings and I submitted our school provistion lists to our dad about two weeks before school began. My dad had his way of cutting down the list: he went from the top of the list with his glasses on, then he'd pick up his old English pen he used for calligraphy to cross out half the list, then he'd call you into his office and say you don't need this and you don't need that, looking above his glasses, and then ask you, "Is this your priority?" He would always, most of the time, give you all the money needed, but he just enjoyed taking us through the process. Dad wanted us to be disciplined and understand what it was to appreciate what we had; sometimes he stretched a little more than was necessary. I always hung around in his office after everyone had gone, then I'd ask him for more money, and most times he'd say, "You have enough," but I would sit at the door of his office or behind the door, making sure I was not visible; on his way out he'd turn and see me lurking around, then he'd say "Child, what do you want?" and I'd smile back at him and say, "I thought you said you would give me

41

more money." At this point, he'd reach into his Agbada and pull out a bundle of crisp Naira and give me a chunk, and then I'd go away happy, telling my other siblings that papa gave me more money! By the time they ran back, my dad would be sitting behind his car wheel and driving off; it would be another four days again before we'd see him.

Usually the driver would take us to the market to buy our provisions. I usually started with the crossed-out items, and my parents would find out a day before I leave for school that I had not picked up any textbooks or exercise books, pencils, sharpeners, and all the priority items that were missing. So, my father would get really mad, give me his famous knock with his ring finger, and then take me to the market and bookstore, and I'd end up with everything on my initial list.

Now the holidays were over and it was time to go back to school. The morning of our leaving home back to boarding school, we ran across the street to our neighbours to say good-bye to our friends. Most of the children went to different schools. Our bags were packed, my father's car's trunk was packed, and Nancy and I were ready to go back to school. My Mom interestingly didn't say much about our school because she was always preoccupied with work and running a home filled with house helps, workers, drivers, cousins, and uncles. She would check to make sure we had all our provisions, and that our uniforms were complete and intact. She'd say good-bye and go back into the house.

The long ride back to school was very quiet—no lectures and no one made a sound. We arrived at the chief matron's house, who went over our list to make sure we had everything we were supposed to come back with. Our pocket money was left with her and our school fees were paid. My dad turned around and said, "Take care of yourselves," and then looked at me sternly and said, "Behave yourself and don't get into any trouble."

We'd say "Yes, sir," and he'd drive off. As I watched my father drive off, warm tears rolled down my eyes and then I broke down and started sobbing. I knew it would be another 3 months before I'd go home again, but then it would be the Christmas holiday.

From a distance, I heard a shrill voice calling out my name: "Ooonnnyyyyeeeejjjjjjaaaaa." As I turned, it was no one but my dear friend Ori. I dropped all I had in my hands and ran to give her a big hug; we laughed and giggled, and we kicked it right off.

My sister had to call me to come back and carry my stuff to the dormitory. That night Ori and I sat up and talked about our holidays and what we did. We didn't travel to fun places like Disney or go to the beach; we spent most of our holidays playing outside, visiting our grandparents, and reading books.

God bless you if you failed; you had extra lessons or private teachers all throughout the holidays. It seened like a lot, but we spent most of our holidays reading; we also had chores. We were still very young and had not started getting the attention of boys, and so we had nothing much to talk about; we talked about our parents and how many times we got into trouble over the holidays; we talked about our end-of-term results and wanted to know who came in first and last in class. I knew for sure I was neither the first nor the last. We talked about all we brought back from home, and how we were going to skip the dining room for the first 2 weeks of school. We had brought back with us Gari (dried cassava flakes), sugar, Kwilikwili (dried peanut sticks hard as rocks), corn flakes, Nasco Biscuits, Milo, and so on. Ori liked Bonvita and powdered milk. We made chocolate from adding Milo and powdered milk with a few drops of water. We stirred it together until it formed a hard chocolate consistency, and we just gulped it down. When we got hungry at lunchtime, we took some gari and added a few teaspoons of sugar and water. It was very satisfying and way better than the food from the school dining room. It wasn't quite 2 weeks when Ori and I ran out of provisions, and we had no choice then but to go back to the school dining room for food.

One afternoon I could not take any more of the boarding school. My sister had missed more classes trying to come out to my class to get me out of trouble or to comfort me from crying. She had had enough, and everyone had had enough. I was out of ideas, so I decided to fall on the floor and act like I had fainted, so I put my hand on my forehead and to the floor I went, then I shook violently; it was amazing how I escaped a scratch. The school matron was called, and everyone started running; the news had gone around that a student had fainted; thank God CPR was not popular back then. In my little 10 and almost 11-

year-old mind, I was excited that it was working, then the school principal showed up and a few teachers; I knew at this point I could not go back on this trick; I had to finish it although I wanted so much to giggle, but I knew that was the end of me if I did. The next voice I heard was my sister's, and the principal told her to take me back home. They had put me in a vehicle and first taken me to a hospital in the small town of Otukpo where my Aunt worked. She was not my aunt per say, but she was married to my Father's older brother. She took a glance at me and just said, "You need to stop. What would you like to eat?" She fed me good and I slept over at her house the following day. My sister and I boarded a train and she took me back to Makurdi, and that was the last of St. Ann's Secondary School. That was also the last I saw of my friend Ori.

In those days, communication was a big deal; we had no computers, or cell phones; we wrote letters that never reached their destination. Until this day, I have searched for my friend and tried to reach her on social media but could not find her.

When I arrived home, my father was on a business trip; he'd be gone one or two weeks at a time. So I had time to prepare for his arrival. My mom said, "Since you do not want an education, you can come and stay right here with me at home." I was just glad to be home. My sister went back to school the following day. I am sure she was glad I was gone at least for a few months. I woke up every day and did nothing for a few weeks because I had left school right in the middle of the term.

My mom sometimes would take me along with her to the hospital where she worked, and she would make me sit down in her office with papers and pencil to write or draw. I loved drawing cartoon characters and comics, while she did her rounds. While I sat in her office, I would go over books and read all the material I could find. She had books on human anatomy and health, and I would draw and color, and when her co-workers came to the office, they were very impressed by the conversations we had, and they always told my mom, "Your daughter is intelligent and has a beautiful smile," and my mom would always chuckle and say, "If only she would stay in school."

At the end of my mom's work day she'd drive us home, and we'd talk about all the women who had babies and what joy it brings to have a healthy delivery and so on, but she never told me about all the women who died at child birth; back then, women died every day from complications from child birth. Women did not get anesthesia for pain control during child birth, and we heard the horror stories outside of our home. Looking over my mother's nursing books, I learned a lot about those risks. In my heart I thought she had a hard job.

We'd stop by the store and pick up bounty chocolate and English tea and Biscuits, and as soon as we got home, I'd run into the kitchen to put the kettle on for my mom's tea. My mother was very much tradtional, but a lot of the English lifestyle rubbed off on her. She was very poised and different from all the other women around her. I admired her so much I wanted to be like her. She dressed nice, and I remember her nursing uniform was always clean and crisp. My mom wore a white nurse's dress with white tights, white shoes, and a cap with round little glasses. She was a petite lady, but always had a presence around her that could not be missed. Everyone loved her; she was very kind and never really spanked us; she left that to my dad. She used her sewing tape to whip me one time, and I screamed like I was being burnt by fire; it felt like paper, but I had to show her she was doing a good job. Most evenings when we arrived home, we had people sitting in the compound waiting for my mom; most of them were men who came in just to say thanks for their wives' safe delivery. They brought yams and palm oil as gifts. My mom gracefully thanked them and accepted their gifts humbly.

My mom took me along with her to work another day and we did the usual routine. Ten minutes after we arrived home on one particular day, my dad came driving into the gates, and my heart sank, not sure what to expect, but I knew for sure the party was over; he had not seen me since I left boarding school.

When my dad came out of the car and saw me, I said, "Anyaa, papa," which simply means "welcome" in Idoma language.

He responded by saying, "This is not you, is it? Don't tell me you came back from school." And for the next thirty minutes he rained down on me; this time he did not touch me, but he walked past me and hissed.

First thing in the morning at the crack of dawn, my dad put me in the car and drove me to the nearest public school, about a ten-minute

47

drive from home. It was called Govennment Day Secondary School, a mixed school for boys and girls. I would have to go in the morning and come home at 4 p.m. My admission and paperwork were done in under ten minutes. I started school again and continued in the same grade I was when I left St. Ann's. I had missed weeks of school, but at this point it was not that important.

My new school was very different; we had boys in the school. We had almost sixty people in one class. If your parents could not afford a desk and a chair, you sat on the floor, and some of the boys sat on window frames. The classrooms had no window glass and no doors; the roof leaked when it rained. I had a locker and a chair; my father called a capenter to make one for me the same afternoon I was enrolled. My uniforms were made by my father's tailor and long-time friend. We nicknamed him "Odear," AKA Udu the Tailor. My father had vowed that none of his children would be without education, so it did not matter what I did; I was going to school.

My first day of school was a reality check: most of the students walked to school, but I was dropped off by our driver. The kids in that school had torn uniforms and others had no sandals; some had very old uniforms that had rips in them. At first, they looked at me funny, and no one wanted to make friends. I didn't know anyone in that school since none of them had attended the same elementary school with me, and most of the students were about a year or two older than I was. Then from behind me, someone called my name; it was a familiar voice. When I turned, it was the house help of one of our

48

friends who attended the same school, and then she asked me, "What are you doing here?"

Then I said, "My dad brought me to attend this school, and I am here now."

She laughed and said, "I hope I can get a ride with you on your way home."

The bell rang, and everyone ran to class; it was not a great environment. The children in that school were angry, and not long before the day was half-way over, a fight broke out between two boys fighting over a stolen biro, or should I say a pen. The teacher broke the fight up and of course sent them out of the class to kneel under the hot blazing sun.

I was adapting to my new-found environment. I did not have to wake up for morning mass, and no one in this school cared about clean uniforms or walking in straight lines, so in all that I was free, but then I was shocked that an environment like this existed around me, and I had no clue. The teachers wrote on blackboards that were almost white; no one had textbooks except for two or three people in the class, and everyone had to come around and share. In my mind I knew I was going home in a few hours. During break time, we ran out of class, and some boys jumped out of the window instead of using the door. We had no water or shops around to buy snacks; you had to wait till you got home to eat. This was obviously not a school for rich and privileged kids, and reality was very much in sight. The children in this school spoke pigeon English even in class, and their teachers were school-teaching-certificate trained, not college graduates. At least not for forms one and two. So, we played at break time. About a week after my being in this school, the boys began to pick on me, but one particular boy (I will call him Eden for the sake of this book.) was very quiet and always kept to himself; he was humble-looking and never bothered anyone.

I noticed he always looked at me during class, and when I turned he would take his eyes away. One day I walked up to him and asked him, "I noticed you always look at me; what do you want?" Bad idea; he was embarrassed by my question, and the other boys thought that was bold of me to have spoken to him like that. He got up and walked out of the class without saying a word to me.

When he finally spoke to me, he said, "I go beat you after school; next time you go think before you come talk to me." He simply said as interpreted that he would beat me up after school and maybe next time I would be wiser not to come up to him again.

I took his threats seriously and walked with the teacher to the staff room until my ride came for me. I completed my first semester in that school and did very well; of course, I was going to school with people who had not learned to read or write early and had not had the luxury of their intellect being stimulated. My parents were pleased that I was in school, but my mother did not think I was getting the best education. I survived one academic year and that was it. I learned my lesson, and it was time for me to move on to a different school and environment. I started to appreciate what I had, but I did not miss my boarding school.

Chapter 4: Tragedy in Our Home

It was December of 1987 that tragedy struck our family. My parents' almost 20 years of marriage was coming to an end. Prior to this year in 1983, my maternal grandmother at the age of 45 became ill and was in Otukpa village, about two and a half hours' drive from Makurdi. My mom woke up early before dawn and rushed to the village to pick her mother up and bring her to the city to receive medical attention. On her way back, somewhere between Otukpo and Makurdi, she had a fatal accident—a head-on collision with an oncoming trailer truck. My mother was thrown out of the vehicle. In that accident her mother died sitting in the back seat, my uncle Steven died, one of our house help died, and only my mother and my uncle Joseph, my father's older sister's first son, survived the accident. Joseph came out with only a scratch on his head. My mother had lost half of her face and was quickly transported to a teaching hospital in Kaduna. We were all taken to the first hospital in Makurdi where she was taken too, to say our good-byes before she was moved; she was in the hospital in Kaduna for six months.

My father had to travel between Kaduna and Makurdi every week to see about my mother's welfare. It was long and hard, and it was taking a toll on my father. The journey between Makurdi and Kaduna ws a good six-hour drive, and all five of us did not know if our mother would ever come back home again. The days were long; we never really talked about the situation. We did a lot of thinking, and I internalized a lot. When my father came home, he always told us our mom was getting better, but we could see the pain in his eyes.

My father and my mother had a bond that was so strong, all our neighbors and friends admired their relationship. I remember growing up, my parents went to late-night parties together; my dad was a sharp dresser and a very handsome man, so all the ladies loved him, and nicknamed him "Guy Man." My mom, on the other hand, was very stylish; she always had on a short skirt or dress with a 5- to 6-inch heel; they were always the life of the party, and always brought us suya when they came back from their late night. My father always smiled or looked at my mom everytime she walked past him, but he quickly turned that smile into a frown when he noticed we were looking at him. Growing up African, men, at least my father, did not show a lot of emotions of love either towards us or my mom. But we knew he loved us; he provided for us and always stood up for us. He never did physically hit my mom and we never saw them argue. They both teased themselves, but it was very subtle; a few times I watched as my parents danced to turn-table music, and we all watched in admiration and laughed and giggled.

Our childhood home was a loving one. My mom spent most of her Saturdays clipping my father's nails and fixing buttons on his shirt; even though we had household help, she wanted to cook and serve his meals. They were both so in love.

But as the months went by, my dad started to struggle a little bit with the stress from my mother lying in the hospital and his not being sure what his future would look like without my mother, so he started to lean more on his friends who took him out to have a good time with a few drinks and loose women. My dad would be gone for a few days at a time. We didn't bother him much; we didn't know what to make of the situation. I was too young to grasp the magnitude of what was going on in my home. One day my dad called us all and said that when my mother had the terrible accident, we had lost our grandmother, and he was going home to do her traditional rights and burial without my mother; it had been too long, and they could not keep waiting. He also said my mother was not aware that her mom had passed away in that accident. He wanted her to heal and then tell her when she got home. We all stayed back in Makurdi when he went to bury his mother-in-law.

My father was close to my grandmother and listened to whatever she told him. And my grandmother loved him too. My dad would drive down to the village every month to take food and provisions to his mother- and father-in-law; he made sure they were taken care of.

I didn't quite understand the magnitude of what my dad just said about my grandmother, but I cried a little; in my little world I knew I would never see my grandmother again. I grew up with her; when my mother was away in school, we spent most of our long vacation with her in the village.

Then I asked my dad, "Will my mom die also?" He turned and looked down at me and said in Idoma, "It's all in God's hands." He then said, "I will leave for Otukpa in the morning and I will see you all when I come back." While he was gone, my older sister Nancy, with house helps and cousins and the other people who lived in our home, was able to make it through the few days my dad was away. Nancy assumed the role of a mother to all four of us, and she had to grow up real fast. In the same season while my dad was in the village buring his mother-in-law, he met my mother's cousin who came to comfort him at the time of his grief, and our sixth sibling and our fifth sister, Rose, was conceived. She was a beautiful baby. This was a big family secret because we did not know about this child until many years down the line.

In the same year about the month of August, my mother had recovered enough to come back home from the hospital, but would be needing a lot of rehabilitation. My dad drove to pick her up, and we were all excited to see her. We waited for her to come home, and as the horn from my father's car went off, we all ran out of our rooms screeming "Mama oyoyo! Mama oyoyo! Mama oyoyo!" which means "Welcome home, momma!" Our neighbors and other people who heard the loud noises came out to welcome her; most people in disbelief that she survived. As my mother climbed down from the vehicle, I noticed she had a veil covering her face, she was thin, and was walking very slowly. She was guided into her room, and as I tried to jump on her, she raised her hands gently to stop me, then her veil came off her face, and I screamed—the right side of her face was gone, her mouth was twisted to one side, she had horrible scars on her face and arms, and her head was bald. My young mind could not contain the image that I had just seen. And tears rolled down her eyes; she was in a lot of pain and could not even open her mouth. She used a baby teaspoon and a little plastic bar to hold her mouth open for a few hours a day. It was a long road to recovery. She continued to gain strength back, and as the months went by her hair started to grow back. She covered the side of her face that was deformed with her hair and dark glasses all day; the bright light bothered her as well. It was about a few weeks after she had come back home that she was told her mother and two others had died in the car accident. She cried even more, and now I can understand the tremendous guilt that she felt through the pain of losing her mother. Momma was only 35 years old at the time.

The accident had done its damage and taken a toll on my parents. I didn't see them talk as much, and my mother had withdrawn. She didn't talk a lot and had few words to say. She had developed migraines and would always ask me for a glass of water to take a headache pill. In more modern times she would have been diagnosed with depression because she had all the classic signs. She was not getting any help mentally, physically, or spiritually.

After one long year, she was strong enough to return to work. She traveled to London a year later for some reconstructive surgery. It did help, but her face was never quite the same. And that affected her self-confidence. My mom stopped going out to her social functions as often and plunged herself into more work and community outreaches with the rural women. I noticed my parents did not speak very often and their relationship had changed.

Business was growing for my dad—he had bcome a contractor, building houses and gathering up estates and lands as much as he could. The demands of work and a growing business were not easy; he started to travel abroad and was beginning to do contracts for Julius Berger, a German company, so he built more houses in the federal capital of Nigeria in Abuja and built houses in Plateau, Kaduna, and Benue states. With this new-found territory in business and wealth, his friends and business partners increased, and everyone wanted a piece of the pie.

It was one afternoon in 1986/87, a few years after the accident, my mother had worked a long day and was taking her regular nap; my sister Nancy was in boarding school and I was still in the government day school; Ofu had just started boarding school in an all-boys Catholic school in Makurdi. Ebowo and Ene were still in elementary school. I had just come back from school and was playing in the compound when the phone rang. I ran and picked it up and said "Hello." The voice from the other end was a female voice that was so deep you had to listen to distinguish if it were male or female. I said "Hello" for the second time and asked, "How can I help you?"

She said, "I need to speak to your mom," and then I replied, "She is taking a nap," and the voice replied, "Tell her Nyeru (This name has been changed for the sake of this book.) needs to speak to her." So, I told her to hold on.

When I went into the room to call my mom, she sprang to her feet and grabbed the phone, and in her sweet but firm voice she said, "Nyeru, how can I help you?" I did not hear what the lady on the other end said, but my mother replied by saying, "I have been married to this man for 20 years; you need to go find your own husband and finish your education," and I heard my mother say clearly, "You are only 23 years old." My mother hung up the phone and went back to her nap, and the only word I heard from her was "Yeye de smell," one of my mom's favorite quotes for "absolute rubbish," or for lack of a better explanation, "filth stinks." She said that a lot, especially when she was angry.

My mother's sister, Lami, had heard the rumor going around that a young polytechnic girl was running around with my father; my Aunty was a thug for a lack of a better word—she would start a fight; it didn't matter who it was, she was never afraid; she was fisty and always wanted to have the last word. She could pick a fight with a baby in the cradle and would hold onto a grudge until kingdom come. She organized her little street friends to shake up Nyeru and her family, just to let them know they were messing with her big sister. Nyeru was attacked on the streets of Kaduna; that was not the most brilliant idea, so while my aunty was rejoicing at her accomplishments, Nyeru

58

called my dad on the phone, and told him that she had called to say hello to my mother in respect, and she sent thugs to beat her up and embarrass her family. At the time in Nigeria, the military had very much power, and in the government, Nyeru was an in-law to one of the top military personnel, and the guy was a military associate to my father's nephew, all of them in high military ranking.

This did not go down well, because my father did not like what he had heard and believed that my mother should not have taken this action. He drove six hours back to Makurdi and asked my mother why she had called Nyeru up to threaten and insult her family. My mother said that she did not call Nyeru, but that Nyeru called the house and I answered the phone; I was the only witness. My father would not hear or believe her, so in his anger he asked my mother to leave his house. Not only was this a strange behavior, my father's face was so different, I didn't understand what had changed.

My mother asked him, "To where do you want me to go to?"

He said, "You will stop asking me by the time I come back from my bedroom." As my dad went into his room, my mom got a little bag and started packing her belongings. We always had people in our home; no one stood up to my dad; no one told him to stop. His very best friend was sitting in the compound when all this was happening. My uncle Godwin, who lived with us, came to my mother's room and started helping her pack her things. Until this day, I could not understand the meaning of what happened that afternoon; I still could not understand the reason for my father's actions. The situation was not enough to have sent my mother away just like that. With nowhere to go and at the age of 35, she was young with 5 children, and now divorced (In my culture, when a man sends his wife away, no papers are needed; it's a divorce.)—the worst thing that could have happened to any woman in that era. Our home would never be the same again. It had changed forever; our home was broken.

As the days went by the reality dawned on me that my parents had separated. I was angry, and a lot of pain came with it. My childhood dream of a family was pulled from under my feet. I was just about becoming a teenager; what was I going to do? How was I going to live without my mother?

My father's countenance had changed toward my mother, and we did not know what the anger was about; he started to hate her and could not stand her. My father was acting as though he was controlled by a force bigger than himself. We were not allowed to visit our mom, especially my brother, because he was a boy. And the boy children could not eat from their mother if she were divorced. Growing up, our parents were not Christians, but served other gods. Most of the gods they worshiped allowed them to swear oaths of fidelity in marriage and the oath/punishment leaned more on the women who could die if they defiled the oath. It was a mess! So, for this reason, my mother could not come close to my dad or enter his house. If we were caught communicating with our mother, we could be disowned, and the male child could die from eating food from his divorced mother. I broke all the rules within the first two weeks of my mother leaving home, and I remember my father telling me he would disown me if I sneaked out one more time to go see my mother. I told him I had no other place to go because I was in my father's house already.

About three months after the Christmas holiday of the year my mother left home, my father married Nyeru in Otukpa village; he threw an elaborate wedding party for his guest, and family, well wishers, naysayers, and whoever cared to attend. I did not attend the wedding and none of my siblings attended. At the age of 23 years old, Nyeru dropped out of a community college, married a wealthy 43-year-old business man, and destroyed and deprived the experiences of five siblings of a joy-filled, loving family.

In the year 1988, Nyeru had finally established herself and had moved into our home; she came with nothing except a box of old clothes. It was very awkward, and the air was so tense we didn't know how to react to this sudden change. My emotions were between shock, anger, and sadness, and I really thought it was a scene from a bad movie or, better still, a dream that I would wake up from and find my mother at my bed telling me all was fine. As the days went by, and the weeks turned into months, I started to realize this was not a dream after all, and there was really no waking up from this one; this has become my reality—a 13-year-old girl that would grow up into a woman someday without the guidance of her mom but a new step-mother. My first move to rebel was not making any plans to go back to school. I was not motivated to do anything. I started to plan in my heart how to destroy this new union that had come to turn my life upside-down. I buried myself into this thought day in and day out until it consumed my entire being; anger and hate with resentment continued to grow. At that age I started to form my perception about men and love and marriage. In my little mind, it was all a lie. I wanted to fight back and get revenge for my mother; little did I know that this union would not need me to annul it; it was just a matter of time.

My siblings and I got very quiet and not very outspoken; we all bottled up our feelings and didn't speak much. Most times we stayed up in our rooms for fear of doing something wrong. My dad was acting very strange and different; he didn't really pay much attention to us. I guess that's the feeling you get when you just married a 23-year-old girl. When we asked questions, we were snapped at or yelled at. Nyeru's voice was not the most soothing; you could mistake her voice for a man. She was about six feet tall with giant feet; she was a scary-looking lady, and you didn't want to get in her way. I didn't see exactly what my dad saw in her.

We call something in Africa remote control or Jazz that was definitely a factor because my dad liked fine women, and she was not one. She didn't know how to cook and most times we couldn't eat her food, but whatever she did that so pleased my dad, he just swallowed all that stinking cassava fufu and slimy soup. She boasted she had taken home economics in high school; maybe if she completed the class, the fufu would at least be cooked.

One night, being the most outspoken kid of all my siblings (and I always paid dearly for my extrovertedness), my mouth went before my thinking; it was dinner time, and when that smelly fufu and soup was given to me, I could not help but say, "This stuff smells; it's not cooked," and I burst out laughing, and all my siblings joined in, and before I knew it everyone expressed themselves in laughter, comments, and jokes across the dinner table till it got chaotic; even the house helps had joined in the laughter. Fufu and soup went flying into the dustbin, and before we knew it, Nyeru had gone upstairs to report the out-of-hands situation to my dad, and he came thundering down the stairs saying, "How dare you make fun of your step-mom and her cooking!" He demanded respect from all of us and threatened to disown anyone who was not ready to comply with his rules. By this time, I had heard that threat too many times to take him seriously, but everywhere was quiet. When my father spoke, you could here a pin drop, then from out of nowhere I could not hold my insides and a laugh came out of me that threw my dad into a fury; he came down on me with a knock that made me hear birds chirp around my head like a halo, with stars in my visual field. Everyone had disappeared into their rooms and the only voice you could here was me crying and walking into my room. The night was pretty much over.

That was the night we came up with a code name for our step-mom. We called her Thatcher, and somedays we switched up and called her Whity because of her light complexion. As children we drafted out plans to use codes that no one else understood except the five of us;

63

we buried our emotions and feelings in much reading, and we sat in our compound singing as sisters. Ofu pretty much played with his friends all the time; he was the only boy among four girls, but our neighbors had five boys, so it all worked out.

Nyeru at this point was trying everything she could to make us like her; she wanted us to sneak out of the house to go visit our friends, and she promised not to tell our father when he came back from his business trips. Somehow our father always found out and we'd get punished, but Nyeru always swore she never told him.

The months went by, and it was time for everyone to go back to boarding school. My older sister went back to her final year in high school; she was now seventeen. And I started a new school about a fifteen-minute drive from home. It was an all-girls boarding school, first called Unity Girls College and then later was changed to Government Girls College. We had to all submit our provision list to our father before resumption as was our usual practice, and Nyeru would stand over my dad making sure the money was allocated and not a penny more. Our overall pocket money was cut in half, and we were not happy campers.

My brother also was going back to boarding school; it was an all-boys Catholic boarding school about 20 minutes away from home. At the time, Ebowo and Eneape were in elementary school and still at home. Nancy, Ofu and I were worried how Ebowo and Eneape would cope with the new change, being so young without mom and their older siblings around; those were very rough times.

Gradually Nyeru being in our home was becoming more difficult to cope with; we were being cut off from our father emotionally. He was always on business trips, and when he was home our step-mom had all the news about all the things we did wrong, except for our 2 younger siblings who probabaly did not know the magnitude of how much their lives had changed. The three of us older siblings were doing very poorly at school, mentally we were exhausted, and I started struggling socially. I could not keep up with the other kids I went to school with. I admired their homes; I wanted to leave my home; I felt so alone. While we played outside with friends, I was careful not to offend anyone because I didn't want any of the kids to make fun of my home situation, so I gradually started to withdraw.

In those days, divorce was not so common, and it was seen as a very bad thing to happen to any family; you could lose your friends. At one point, we stopped getting all the frequent birthday invitations; families didn't want to associate with us any more. It looked like our home was being talked about by everyone else. My father was quite popular in the community. We had no hiding place. To make matters worse, we had our home filled with many relatives, cousins, and aunts who lived with us and went to school; at the time we were younger, and they were in high school and college. When my mother left home, they all supported my dad because that was the only way they could get their needs met, tuition paid, and a future, so they did all they could to be a watchman for our father; they always told on us for no reason, they ran errands for Nyeru, and made sure they had the best grades in school.

One particular cousin of ours took the place of our firstborn and did all she could to become best friends with Nyeru; they shopped and went to the open market together, they were also close in age, about one to two years apart; she got more pocket money for school, and my father praised her all the time; she could never do anything wrong. Everyone came and took advantage of the situation; the drivers and house help all joined in until we became like strangers in our father's house. We could never do anything right, we could never make the best grades, and we could not clean or act right. When it pleased my dad, he took us to traditional meetings where parents took their stubborn youths who were reprimanded for bad behavior or if your grade was poor. The meeting was called "the Obekpa youth club." We would be dragged right into the middle, and everyone had something to say about our behavior. By this time enough emotional damage was done that it was hard to trust anyone in our home. And by the end of the first year of Nyeru coming into our lives, we had started having physical fights. She had long sharp nails she painted red, the same color as her lipstick; if I remembered, her nail polish was Theons Nail Lacquer and the lipstick was pepper red in color; that red lipstick stayed on for 24 hours and stained every cup in the house. One day she was in a physical altercation with Ofu when she clawed him in the face with those nails; his skin was torn from the bottom of his eye down to his cheek; it's been a good 38 years, and those marks still run deep in his face. My father then came out to see what was going on, and for the first time in a long time my father was very upset; that was his son and he would not take that nonsense. He straightened everyone out and sent everyone to their rooms. We had a family meeting, and at the time a decision was made that everytime we came back from boarding school, we would have to go to Jos in Plateau, about five hours from our family home in Makurdi, to spend our holidays to avoid conflict and trouble. At the house in Jos, we would have a cook, a driver, and a housekeeper. And all five of us were sent up north and came back home only for the Christmas holidays.

After Ebowo completed her elementary school, she was sent to middle and high school in Jos at the Federal Government college; it was a bording school, and Eneape was sent off to boarding school as well, to a Federal Government girls' secondary school in Gboko, so all five of us were in boarding schools at different locations and came together for only 3 months in the year, and so we did grow apart. We all had different experiences when we were home and, depending on your character or personsality, you had a different treatment. We all plunged into school and gave it our all, and we derived a lot of satisfaction in so much education. I didn't care much, but I managed to scratch by.

Communication with my mother was getting more difficult; we could not see her or talk to her as was the custom; nothing of hers could be brought into our home, and she could not come into my dad's presence or come into any of his properties because of the consequences of aleku (dead god). We believed all that lie until the yearning for our mom was becoming overbearing. I would cry at night; I would yearn for her touch and soft-spoken voice. I missed her stories and her cooking; I missed everything she brought into our home.

My life was changing before my eyes; I could not bear it any more, and the impossible happened. I broke all the rules and sneaked out of the house one day. I was supposed to be going to school, but I went to spend the day with my mother. I did not get any transportation for fear of being seen and caught. I followed the train tracks that led through plaza hotel; she was staying at a rented apartment that a friend of hers had given her and was somewhere close to the hospital where she worked. It was a good forty-five-minute walk. When I got to the gate, I looked at my left and right, and I looked behind me to make sure no one had seen me. It was amazing how, back then, you could be walking, and some random person would call you out and ask where you were going as if your parents knew you were out! How the world has so changed! So as I stood in front of this black gate, I hit the gate as hard as I could, and I heard this tiny voice from behind in my native language ask, "Who is it?"

I could not say my name for fear of someone else hearing me, so I responded "Mama," and immediately she opened the gate; I ran into her arms and she quickly took me inside, and I went straight for the

68

pot. She had fixed Jollof rice and chicken; my mom was an excellent cook. We talked and cried, and she said she was sorry for leaving us like that, but it was beyond her control. I was now fourteen years old, and what came out of my mouth was "Mama, papa said if I ate from you I would die; is that true?"

She responded, "I am not sure about that, but according to the custom, yes, but don't worry, nothing will happen to you; it's worse for the male children."

I don't know what was funny in all she said, but I laughed and had a witty answer. "Well, I am still alive, and it doesn't look like I'm going to die; can I go get some more?"

She smiled and said "Sure, but hurry up; we need to catch up on jist (everything)." We had so much to catch up on and not enough time; she wanted to know how all five of us were doing and how we could arrange a meeting. I told her I didn't know how that could work, but we could make it happen.

She wanted to know all about Nyeru and how she treated us. Of course, I told her all that was going on and about the smelly food and slimy soups. My mom and I had a good laugh. I had so many good memories.

She started to tell me and teach me about the lessons of life and about men; she wanted to know if I had a boyfriend. Out of her hurt came not so great advice about men, which advice at the time I thought was the best thing in the world. She said that men were not worth fighting for; they didn't care much, and they never got hurt; they would always find someone better or younger. "So, don't fight in the street and mess your face up. It's not worth it."

My sneaking technique became more often, and my skipping school also was increasing. One day I got back home from one of my trips, and my father was sitting in the middle of the compound waiting for me. I had stayed too late and forgot that the time had gone by so fast.

It was the same evening my mom had told me she was tired of the humiliation and the stigma of leaving her five children for a younger woman and being kicked out. She said she had decided to leave Nigeria and go to Saudi Arabia to look for work and provide for herself. She said she would make more money out there as a nurse mid-wife and would sign a three-year contract, and maybe things would work out between her and my dad. At the time I knew Saudi Arabia was in the Middle East, but I didn't know how far it was. I just cried because an overwhelming sadness came over me, and I knew this was going to be another change I was not prepared for.

While I was contemplating all these thoughts, the gates opened, and my father's voice welcomed me. "Where are you coming from? I need you to tell me where you are coming from."

My brain had stopped for a minute. Then I stuttered and said, "From mama's place."

He got up on his feet and said, "What did you just say?"

"I said I am coming from my mama's house."

From the top of his lungs my father said in his favorite words, "Are you crazy? I have been watching you and they have told me where you have been going. If you ever leave this house again to see your mom, I will disown you. Here we go again, and you will leave my house."

Then I grumbled back to him, "But this is my father's house; your father's house is in Otukpa village," and that ticked him off. He got up and followed me, but I knew better when to run, and I was gone. I escaped that night to tell my story another day.

When it quieted down, my siblings came to ask me about mama, and I told them all that we had talked about. I told them she wanted to see all five of us, and I told them her plans of leaving the country to go to Saudi Arabia. We all tried to come up with a plan to make that happen before it was time to go back to school, but we didn't want anyone to hear us so we all went to bed. The walls in our home at the time had ears.

The only way my mom could come see us at the time was to come over to our neighbor's house, so we went across to see her. It was not so comfortable knowing that we had our neighbours watching and listening to our conversastion while we visited with our mom; it was humiliating and not the most pleasant, but we cherished every moment. All five of us had our turns to talk to her and catch up on stories. Not too long afterwards, we heard our names being called to come back home, and we knew exactly who it was and why we were been called. We said our good-byes and, one after the other we cried and let go; it was more difficult for me to let go.

That night I was so turned on the inside, and I had so much on the inside of me I wanted to talk to my mom about alone, but I just couldn't with everyone present. I wanted to tell her the struggles I was having in school, and my struggles making real friends and being afraid of the rejection I received from the situation in our family. I felt so alone; I needed my mom, but she was not there. I was at the age when I needed to be affirmed and encouraged, I was at the age when I needed to be told I was growing up as an intelligent young girl, and I was at the age when I needed someone to listen to my dreams and plan about what I would like to become. I had dreams of places I would love to visit, but so many dreams all drowned in the pain of a broken home.

Chapter 5: My Mother Relocated to Saudi Arabia

My mother officially told my other siblings about her leaving for Saudi Arabia, even though I had already told them. She had signed a three-year contract with an agency in Saudi Arabia to work as a nurse midwife, so she left for Saudi Arabia and communication became more difficult; we would not see our mom again except one time a year for about three days at Easter; at Christmas she would send us a Christmas card that she had risked her life to buy from an underground shop.

She wrote very sweet letters and expressed her pain in most of her letters, and as I read the words of the letters she wrote, I would cry and long for my mother. She wanted me to update her on what was going on in our home; we had our little code words; she knew she could rely on me to give her all the details, and she had so many questions about my dad and wanted to know how he was doing. I knew my mother still loved my dad and cared deeply for him. She wanted to know how our step-mom treated us and she always told me to listen and not be stubborn to my step-mom. I did really try to heed that advice because the more letters I read, the more pain and sorrow filled my heart, and I was hurting for my mom and wanted to pay back every wrong that was done to her.

My life completely turned around; I lost interest in playing with friends and doing what typical teenagers do; I buried my life in the world of fantasies as I spent time reading books, novels, magazines, and whatever I could lay my hands on to read.

I didn't like the romance novels at the time, even though I read a few—it was popular that all the girls read Mills and Boone; I hated it; it was boring in my opinion. I lived in Nigeria; I could not connect the identity of men with pale skin, blue eyes, and long, braided hair riding on a horse with the wind and all that. The writer used a chapter to describe the masculine features of the male character; the boys and men I saw around me didn't look anything like the novel; they had brown skin baked in the sun with crinkly hair. The romance novels were not comprehensible, and the women portrayed in those books were appalling; I could not understand all the emotions they expressed towards the male character. I could not see the book in my parents' marriage, and at that point I concluded that those romance novels were lies, so I dumped them.

On the contrary, my older sister, Nancy, had over one hundred romance novels, and she loved them, and she had a collection of country music as well. She loved Dolly Parton and Kenny Rogers. I read history books, adventure books, and comic books; I read the average teenage boys' comic books, I read books by John Grisham, and I started reading mystical books, and the list went on and on. I listened and danced to Michael Jackson and spent my time learning how to sing every new release. We occupied ourselves with all and everything.

Not long after mom had traveled to Saudi Arabia, my father welcomed the birth of his second son, the seventh child of our family. Our family started to grow bigger—for Nyeru, that was an accomplishment and stability for her in the home, as male children were a prized possession and valued in the Nigerian culture. With the birth of Nyeru's son, she became a force to be reckoned with. She gained favor in the sight of my dad and all his relatives and cousins and drivers and maids. All five of us became more like outsiders in our own home. And the misery got worse. We stopped talking as much as siblings, and we all found what we liked to do and did it.

At this point, my school situation got so bad I was changed to an all-girls boarding school, and at the time it was a new school that had just started. We were about a total of 300 girls in the school, and we were the first set; it was a junior secondary school. I was in JSS 3, and that was my third secondary school. I was in a different school every year.

My dad at this point had had it and didn't know what else to do with me.

The morning of our Assembly before classes, the principal of my school had decided all the girls should shave their hair to no longer than one inch, because she wanted us to do well in school and not focus on braiding and plaiting our hair. That didn't go down well with me or any of the girls, so after school was over that day, I decided to rally a few girls in my corner at night, and we came up with a plan on how to organize a rally to the government house to fight for our right to keep our hair from being cut. All the girls cheered me on because they thought it was a brilliant idea; some said, "Who is this girl who just came to our school and has the nerve to organize such a courageous act?"

I guess all the books and pain of my home was about to unleash itself. As excitement mounted, about 5.30 a.m., I sent a few of the girls into the different dormitories to wake everyone up and assemble at the Emerald house dormitory. All the girls in the school were divided into four different groups: we had Ruby house, Topaz, Sapphire, and Emerald house. I was the Dormitory prefect for Emerald house. All the girls got together, about 250 of them. I addressed the girls, and urged them to stand for what they believed in; shaving our hair was demeaning. After about 30 minutes of prompting and encouraging the girls, we came up with a song, and with me leading the way, we marched out of the school gate and out onto the main roads. It was a sea of heads, at that time that was very strange to see a bunch of 12-, 13- and 14-year-old girls with our school uniforms on, on a weekday stopping traffic and marching to the Government house for a stupid cause.

Not long into the march the school principal got wind of what was happening and activated the police; before I knew what was happening, a simple march had turned into a full-blown riot; girls were running everywhere, and the police were chasing us down; cars stopped in traffic all the way from the Government girls' campus to the streets and beyond. Adrenalin was rushing high; I wasn't even thinking I was so excited, but then in a flash I realized what I had done, and just the thought of my father finding out was unnerving. O well, I figured it was too late now. I managed to make it back to my dormitory without been caught. I ran as fast as I could, but it was not so for the other girls; a lot of them were cut and taken to the police station, and the news was everywhere. When parents started arriving at the school and wanted to find out what had happened, the principal of the school called for a disciplinary team to handle the situation. Most of the girls were brought back to school safely, and a few stayed back and never left the campus.

The next morning, a few girls were called to the principal's office, and I was among the ten. With no questions asked we were all suspended for two weeks. Most of the girls were crying, and I knew for a few of them that that was the end of school, and their education was one shot for them, although in this time and age, people would wonder what such a big deal it was in what we did! It was a big deal knowing that in that era and in the African culture, to bring disgrace to your family and home due to bad behavior was not acceptable. Education was an investment and not free. For some had come very far from different states and would not go back home for a two-week suspension, so they made plans to stay with a friend, then return to school.

As I left the principal's office, I saw a car that looked like one of my father's cars, and a driver was waiting for me. I knew in my heart if I didn't die today, I would live to see many more years. My father had gotten wind of the story, had seen the story, and then was told his daughter had led a school riot. My dad was the only parent who came to the school to apologize; he knew I had disgraced him and the family name.

When I arrived home, as the first point of punishment, my father took a blade and shaved my hair to the scalp—you could see your reflection on my scalp—and he shaved my eyebrows too. My father said, "If you would lead a school riot for a foolish reason as braiding your hair, I guess if you don't have any hair on your head, you won't be thinking of braiding it." My dad did a good job with the shaving because my hair was coarse and thick; it was so painful, I could only grunt; I didn't have the courage to cry. When he finished shaving my hair, he looked at me and said, "You are home for two weeks; I do not want to see your face or hear your voice until you return back to school; if the principal will not accept you back, I will have to go see her personally."

When my dad walked away from me, I turned around to go to my room, and when I turned all my brothers and sisters looking through the window all started laughing at the same time; then at that point, hot balls of tears began to roll down my cheeks. I ran and grabbed a mirror, I looked like an alien from Mars. I had no eyebrows and no hair, and because I was stick thin it looked even worse; I had all kinds of bumps and ridges on my scalp, then I actually realized I was looking at my scalp for the first time; my head was actually big. Then

I cried the more, not from remorse from what I did in school, but from the humiliation of losing my hair.

Not long after my hair was shaven, I started finding ways how to make my hair grow quickly because I knew I had to go back to school in two weeks and face my schoolmates, so I started applying alcohol on my scalp and whatever I could find to enhance my hair growth; nothing worked. Two weeks went by quickly, and the morning of my going back to school, I woke up early. I had not slept all night, and the humiliation of going back to school with a bald head and no eyebrows was not a joke, but I knew that was the last time I was going to do anything stupid in my father's house; there was too much of a price to pay.

While I was still thinking, I heard my father's voice: "ON-YE-JE," and I answered, "Sir?"

My dad replied back, "I will be leaving here by 7 a.m., and you better be ready. I don't want you to miss assembly." Just when I thought the humiliation was over, my dad wanted to take me to school while the students were lined up outside for assembly. If I could have disappeared, I would have. I dressed up quickly after a quick shower; I bet I left one foot unwashed. I wore my uniform, knee-high socks, and Bata sandals. With my bags packed and no single strand of hair on my head or eyebrows, I could not look in the mirror; I greased my scalp with Dax pomade and hopped into the back seat of my dad's car. I was hoping the driver would drop me off, but my dad insisted on taking me himself.

My dad took a good look at me and he broke out in a laugh and said, "My friend, sit up; your head (makes you) look like a recruit." It was a long drive to school, and my dad talked the whole way as was his manner, telling me how I disgraced his family name and how I needed to focus in school and so on. By the time the gate opened, and my dad pulled into the school compound, the bell was ringing, and everyone was running to the assembly ground. My dad pulled up and asked me to come out of the car. I could not move. Then he said for the second time, "My friend, get down; next time you'll think twice before you start another school fire."

I said, "Papa, I did not start a fire."

He said, "Whatever you started, get down and run to the assemble ground and tell your principal I said hello."

By the time I made my way to the ground, my principal raised her squirky voice and said, "Here she comes, welcome back!" and the whole assembly roared with laughter.

As I made my way to the line, she told me to come up there, and as I walked up the stairs to the platform, it got quieter with a few giggles, and I could see my teachers shaking their heads and whispering to each other. By the time I got close to my principal, she said, "Welcome back, Onyeje Obekpa!"

For some reason, everyone called me by my first and last name like it was one name. I looked at her and put my face back to the floor, and she started laughing; that was when I knew I must really look crazy and funny for my principal to be laughing.

She said, "Girls, I want to commend Prince Obekpa for the discipline he has given to Onyeje; she has come back to school changed and is ready to learn. She looks so beautiful with her hair like this." My comical side came back, and I rubbed my head with my hand and gave a surprised look; for a minute I thought my hair had grown back, and everyone started laughing. Then she said, "But it looks like she's still clowning."

I walked down to my class and, being a little taller than most of my classmates, I stood at the back of the line. We proceeded to singing the national anthem, announcements and inspections, and of course my bags were checked before I could check into my dormitory later on that day. We used to sneak in canned goods and just a list of things we could not bring from home.

I was so happy when the day was over; all the girls wanted to find out what my two weeks' suspension was like with my father. Everyone knew my dad was strict, and we stayed up all night and talked about it, and as the days went by things became normal again; by the fourth week, I had hair on my head, and my eyebrows had grown back pretty quickly.

I was part of the debate club, and I skipped a few appearances because I could not go to the other schools to compete because I just could not face the opposing school without my hair. I remember we would go to the Boys' school, and this time my school had lost. We had a strong team. I remember it was Vivian, Etim and I. We loved to debate and argue our case for or against the topic given. We won all the time; we debated with boys from Government college in Makurdi, but the Mount Saint Gabriel boys were always a challenge, and they always put up a good fight. I was very active in the drama and debate clubs in school, and we traveled around locally to perform. That kept my mind away from reality, and I was good at what I did. Not long afterwards, I was in the local newspaper for a play we acted in: The Lion and the Jewel by Professor Wole Soyinka. I was Lakunle, a school teacher in the play that fell in love with Sidi, the beautiful village girl. We had opportunity to meet with state governors and present plays in the art and culture theater.

At the time I turned 16, I was beginning to like a mulato boy who was a hothead and a good science student at St. Gabriels; he was in a boarding school and I was in a boarding school; we could not visit each other, but we did exchange letters, and during the holidays we would talk over the phone when my dad traveled on a business trip. That didn't last too long because he was seventeen and completed high school and went on to university in Ibadan and started a different life.

I was completing high school right about this time. I wasn't doing very well in my academics because all the extra-curricular activities in school were taking up all my time, and I was faced with the question of what I wanted to do when I got to university. I was not prepared to take any standardized test; I had no clue how I was going to achieve this goal to pass JAMB scores to go to the University of my choice. My dad was very concerned as he had high hopes for all of us, and college was not a choice; it was a must. We all had to be Doctors, Lawyers, Engineers, or at least an Accountant. Singing, dancing, and acting, to mention a few careers, were not considered in my home and most African homes at the time as a career; you were labeled irresponsible, lazy, or dumb. You might get a whipping for trying to pick the other choices; it was taboo to be a musician, so you sang in church, in school, in the shower, on the playground, or when you cried, but that was it.

My dad hired private teachers to teach me and prepare me for my WAEC and JAMB; I had the best teachers. My dad was determined to whip my brain into a scientist in four months, critically thinking and processing at the speed of light during my long vacation (summer break). My dad had hired this short guy from Australia (I can't remember his name; I'll call him John.) to teach me math. His accent was all I listened to when he taught me calculus, then I had Mr. Chuku May (his soul rest in peace) who taught me physics, and he taught math and physics at St. Gabriels Catholic secondary school. He was very smart and had a bunch of students coming to him for private lessons. Half the time he talked to me about how good Otukpa palm wine was.

Then I had Peter Julian, my chemistry teacher from Trinidad and Tobago; he was a tall, handsome Catholic priest. At the time he was about 24; I'm not sure what he was thinking when he answered the call to be a Catholic priest. I really would like to know where and what happened to him today. Anyway, I remember when I had chemistry lessons, our driver would take me to St. Gabriels, and just behind the older building, my chemistry teacher had a humble apartment with no TV, one room and pots, a table and a chair and another chair for me to sit on. I came in with my huge Ababio chemistry textbook, and I believe that was the only textbook used at the time. I brought mine and he had his, and, looking through the window, my father's driver was parked half asleep in the car waiting for my one-hour lesson to be over.

I didn't have a lot of one-on-one interactions with boys because I went to boarding school, and my father would not tolerate those types of interactions, so it was very odd for me to be sitting with Peter Julian. I remember leaving lessons, and all I could think about was this priest. Then I started looking forward to going to lessons. As I went back to my chemistry lessons the next day, I remember just like yesterday he was teaching me about solving a problem using the periodic table, and while he was talking he raised his head up, and I was just staring at him; he took the pencil he had in his hand and tapped me on my head and said "CONCENTRATE; what are you looking at?"

Then I said, "You." I was sixteen, but I was very bold; I was not shy but spoke my mind before thinking.

I could see that he had a smile in the corner of his face, but being a priest, and trying to be firm, he got a hold of his rosary in his left hand and said, "Lesson is over for today. Mass begins in fifteen minutes. Complete your homework, and I will see you next week. All those teachers were great! A little boost to my grades, but I still did not make the cutoff point. I graduated high school, but I didn't get to my first choice of the University of Ibadan, but I was able to get into remedial studies in the University of Jos, in preparation for the medical program.

Chapter 6: First Year of University

I was so excited that I was going to University, because not so many people got the same opportunity. My mother was excited when I told her the news. She had come home for Easter from Saudi Arabia, and I was supposed to start school the fall of the same year. My older sister was attending the same university I was planning to attend; I had cousins who attended the same university. I was born in that city, and my family had lived there for a while. Now I would be going five hours away from home. I had graduated in May and turned 17 in June. My dad had high hopes, and we all were ready. In August my dad drove me and my sisters to Jos, and we had a beautiful home in Rock Haven. My sisters and cousins wanted to stay on campus, but I chose to stay home to enjoy the amenities. I was the child who did not want to be stretched; my father had a cook, a driver, and a housekeeper named Micheal. Micheal was loyal to my dad for many years. He came to our house when I was in primary school, and now I was in university. My dad had left a car in the garage, but you dare not touch that car or else you were gone from this earth. The house in Rock Haven was my father's luxurious pad where he came to spend time with his friends and business partners. We used the home for vacation, but now that we were going to university in the same city, we could call it our home off campus. I was off campus; the rooms on campus were small and nasty, and I didn't like the common showers.

It was the first day on campus. Jos was cold—it was September and about 52 degrees but felt like 20 degrees coming from Makurdi.

As was my father's usual tradition, he packed us up in his car: my cousin, my older sister, and I; our school luggage was in another vehicle with the driver. Because of the size of our family, we never traveled anywhere in one vehicle, it was always in two or three vehicles, and one or two children were always left behind for not passing an exam or just punishment for being disobedient.

We arrived in Jos and drove straight to Rock Haven, a beautiful estate. His house in Rock Haven was a fun house and one of the most beautiful houses he ever owned: the ceilings were beautiful, the furniture was intricately designed; long, luxurious curtains draped to the floors; all the fixtures were hand-picked; it had a 2-car garage; boys' quarters where the housekeeper and cook stayed, fenced all around; coming out of the huge, black, metal gate, you could see beautiful rocks—the landscape was breathtaking. Adjacent to the dining area was a bar; my dad had collections of wines from all over the world from his many travels.

When we arrived, Papaa the cook (He looked about 65 years old.) ran outside the compound to welcome and greet us; he had prepared a meal for us and had set the dining table. We were all tired and hungry and had been traveling for about 5 hours. My dad was very proud of his handiwork and showed us around the building. We sat down at the table to eat, and when I opened the plate, Papaa our cook had fixed liver pudding, chicken alakat, and some vegetables that had no name. We all started laughing and asked for jollot rice or fufu.

My dad replied with a smile that this is continental; the cook had taken his time to make this dish. We all had a good laugh, and my sister being the cook, threw some rice in the pot with tomatoes. We thanked Papaa for his effort and were pleased that he made the food.

We all stayed up very late; it was a very cold night and I couldn't get comfortable. We had no room heaters; we made do with blankets. In the morning my dad was ready to leave back to Makurdi, so he called us and gave us his talk about what was allowed and what was not. He instructed us on our new journey and finally ended his speech with "No Boyfriends." My sister and cousins opted to live on campus, but I chose to stay home.

A week went by, and I started going to school late every day. It was hard for me to walk to the bus stop and catch a taxi. The house was 2 drops from campus; I had to get a cab from Rock Haven, to Farengada or Gada beu, and then another cab to university at Jos campus.

In my first few days on campus, I had already made new friends. I met an Igbo girl who was very kind and wanted to become a friend and a sister. We had started the remedial programs together. The classrooms were so packed we never made it on time to get a seat in the class. People stood on the lockers at the back and held their notebooks in their hands to write, while others looked through the windows and pressed in just to listen to the lecture.

I remember one morning in a biology class, the class had over 100 students and we could not all find a spot, so we formed our own group outside and called it section two. We sat outside on the pavement and talked while lectures went on. The weeks turned into months, and that became my lecture hall outside the class. I had made a couple of friends at this time that enjoyed that group; that group of students was now becoming popular. I was the odd one out because I just came from a home where you did nothing to join a bunch of seventeen-, eighteen-, and nineteen-year-olds with lots of stories and experiences, and I admired all of them and wished I had the boldness they had if not for my father's voice behind my ears. The group of students that would hang outside the class included me, Ify, 2-face, black face, one group member of the plantation boys, and a whole bunch of people whose names I can't remember now.

Thinking back, all those friends talked about their dreams and aspirations; none of us belonged in that pre-med class, but we all made it in because our parents felt we all had to be doctors, or nothing else. Some of those people today went on to become songwriters, actors, journalists, musicians, and so on. By the second month on campus, I had missed my first tests in physics, and one day while I was sitting outside with my group, my uncle at the time who was the head of the medical school at Jos University Teaching Hospital (JUTH), Professor Obekpa, was walking by, and I tried to run and hide; I was too tall and stood out in every crowd. He called me by my name with a loud voice, and I ran up to him. He said, "So this is where you sit out here with rifrafs. I am going to call your dad today and let him know you are not in school." I went down on my knees and started pleading; he walked away and asked me to come by his house after school that day. When I turned around to go back to my group, not even one of them was left; we had respect for authority.

The semester had gone by so quickly and I could not account for what I had achieved in school; my grades were so poor my father threatened to disown me; my father had threatened to disown me more than I can count. Then, it was not fun. I begged and asked for a second chance, and by January of the following year, I was eighteen years old and would be turning nineteen the same year. My father was getting very worried about my academic situation. Coming back to school, the group had thinned out; some of the students never made it back; they had pursued other universities. Others had gone to pursue their music dreams and, oh well, the rest of us made it to class when we could.

One morning after lecture was over, a four-hundred-level medical student, Chima, was waiting outside my class and wanted to meet me. His father was a friend to my uncle; he wanted to see if I would go out to lunch with him. I said no, but we walked around the campus together. He was older than I was—twenty-three years old at the time. I didn't know how to handle what he had asked me. I was excited, but not quite sure. Two weeks passed, and it was going to be Valentine's Day. Chima asked me if I would go out to dinner with him, and I asked my uncle if I could go. My uncle gave me permission to go, but asked Chima to bring me home by 7 p.m. Chima came to pick me up at 5:30, and we went to a restaurant at Ahmedu Bello Way. We had burgers, and Chima talked about his big dreams of finishing medical school and moving to the United States, and wanted me to come with him, and asked me if I would be his girlfriend. I wasn't quite sure what was going on in my mind. I chuckled; it was a silly chuckle, the same chuckle that gets me in trouble all the time; it didn't have a real meaning to it, but I guess it was my way of saying no, or maybe a better answer than silence. I chuckle when I am uncomfortable or when I am being silly. Chima looked at me in confusion and asked me, "What does that mean? Is that the answer to what I just said?"

Then I chuckled even more. We didn't have that conversation again. I swallowed my burger so fast I wanted to go home. We were back home a little before 7; it was a quiet drive back home. When we pulled into my uncle's driveway in Road Six, at the lectures quarters, my cousins were looking through the window, not sure what they wanted to see, but I walked into the house and my cousin Linda ran up to me and started asking me questions. "Did he try to kiss you? Are you his girlfriend?" and so on. My cousins were in high school and I was in university. I love them all so dearly; I turned to my cousin and laughed: "Those Romance novels you're reading are getting into your head." As I walked pass her, I said, "I really need to go to sleep."

That was it. I never saw Chima again. Until this day, I wonder where he is today. (I hope you're able to read this book. You were such a gentle man. I forgot to say 'thank you' for the Burgers.)

Little did everyone around me know that I was missing my mother, and that created a lot of void in me, and because my parents had a failed marriage, I did not have any interest in dating. I was hurt and didn't know how to act with the opposite sex. I wasn't sure how to respond to them. I did honestly believe they were evil. I kept a smile, and when the young girls went to parties or started dating, I wanted to keep everybody on the surface, at least if they didn't know what I was dealing with, I didn't have to worry about explaining myself. I told myself, when I was ready, I would just find someone; love was not real and did not exist.

I started getting more popular on campus for no reason; some people around me thought I was funny and had very witty comments. I could hold a little crowd and have them listen to my jokes and comical ways.

A lot of boys wanted to know this girl who came from Makurdi. I didn't have a boyfriend, and to everyone who asked me out I said no, and the general opinion was that I was trying to be exclusive or proud. One day a guy, who was a member of the university fraternity, came out to see who I was; they nicknamed him Nonso—he was a notorious boy and was known for carrying a gun on campus. I was sitting outside in front of the remedial building when he walked up to me and said, "Hello."

I looked up, and when I saw his dental arrangements, AKA jagged teeth, I chuckled and laughed so hard, he told me not to come to school the next day. O well, I didn't make it to school that time, for as I was on my way, news had broken out that there was a riot on campus between the student union and cult boys. It was common in most universities in Nigeria; they had a lot of riots on campus, and lecturers would go on strike two weeks before the end of a semester and come back a year later; it was a mess.

I ended up making friends with the neighborhood girls and boys who were up to no good; a lot of them had graduated high school and didn't get into college because of a very low WAEC (West African Examination Council) score, and they walked around the streets. Some of the girls were in high school and came from very complicated home situations.

I met this girl, Chichi; her father was in the military, and they lived beside our house. I admired her because she had the freedom to do whatever she wanted. She even smoked cigarettes; that was a big deal at the time. I was older than she was, and she was in senior secondary three. She had long nails, long hair and was very pretty; she had a boyfriend, too.

One day Chichi said to me, "You're too conservative; your parents are not here, and you can do whatever you like. I have a party on Saturday, and I want you to come and meet all my friends."

On the day of the party, I dressed up in my blue jeans and a simple blouse. I didn't have heels, so I threw on my loafers. I had a six-inch afro pinned to the side. No makeup, just plain; I was so green. When I got to the party, she held my hands and started introducing me to everyone in the room. She spoke with a very fake British Igbotic accent: "Meet my friend Onyeje; she lives across from us, and she is at the University of Jos and doesn't have a boyfriend." The music was so loud I just kept smiling at everyone and nodding my head. Then the DJ changed the music, and I noticed everyone jumped to their feet and started nodding their heads and waving their hands. They were dancing to Snoop Doggy Dog's *six million ways to die*, and Doctor Dre. I turned around to make a little movement and I bumped into a boy, and when I raised my head it was none other than Nonso. My feet went numb and I could not move. I thought that was my last day on earth! He said, "Hello, onyyen-jey," and all I could see were those teeth, but this time I had no chuckle but a gaze of horror, and it dawned on me that this could be a set up. I didn't even know anyone there; our housekeeper and the cook didn't even know when I left the house.

Then from behind me, another voice came, and a fellow took my hands and said, "Hello, my name is Silvester, but everyone calls me Sly," and he nudged Nonso to step aside, and then he asked, "Are you new? We live down the street from here, and I have seen you walk down a couple of times." He looked very normal and was very friendly; he said, "If you ever need someone to walk you down to the bus stop or walk you home, let me know."

And I said, "Thank you."

Chichi appeared and pulled me aside and said, "Here is a cigarette; try it; it won't hurt."

I said to her, "My father would kill me if he finds out, and besides he said I will go mad if I smoked a cigarette. My father always told us that the Obekpa children did not smoke, and a curse would be upon anyone who smoked a cigarette—they will definitely go mad."

Chichi laughed and said, "That's not true."

So, what did I do? I took the cigarette, lit it up and smoked it; I didn't cough or choke, and I didn't die or go mad. I felt like Eve in the Garden of Eden—my eyes were opened; all my dad's threats were lies to keep me and my siblings from going wild. Well it worked all these years.

It was getting very late and I had to go back home. Now I had the boldness to talk to Sly to walk me home, because I'd just discovered that my father would not find out if a boy walked me home. Sly was delighted and walked me home. Sly was a boy who did not go to college and stayed home; he was the last son of an ambassador to the United States. His siblings were well educated and had their early education in America.

Sly was very comfortable at home, and we became friends. He walked me to the end of the street to catch a cab to school and waited for me at the bus stop to walk me back home. Sly and I became very close

95

friends, and my feelings were going towards him when reports reached my dad in Makurdi that I was being escorted by some guy.

My dad was in Jos and at home before I got back from school; he didn't tell me he was coming. I opened the gate after saying goodbye to Sly. I walked into the compound and there my father was standing, looking straight at me, furiously; I can never forget that day. He told me how dumb and inconsiderate I was in every vocabulary he could find! Oh, he was angry! He said he obtained information and he could not remember the last time I was in school; my world was just beginning to crumble. This was what I feared the most. I never wanted to be confronted by my dad; he was a very tough man.

By the time I woke up in the morning, he was gone; he never left any money for me and never said goodbye; he was gone. At the time there were no cell phones, so I could not call him. I wrote an apology letter—that was our usual practice when we did something wrong— we wrote letters and promised not to make the same mistakes, and my dad would file those letters and keep them as a reminder for repeat offenders.

I did not see Sly again. I sent Micheal the housekeeper to tell him that my father was very upset with me and would kill me if he ever found out I was sneaking out of the house or walking the street with him. I'm not sure if the message was given or not; I know I never saw him again till this day. (I wonder where you are today; I hope something good came out of your life.)

Chapter 7: My Mother's Death

It wasn't too long after my dad had left, after I had just spent 2 semesters in UJ, and the end to the second semester was aproaching, that I was walking on campus one morning when a student that knew my family said to me, "Sorry about what happened to you; I heard the news."

Then I said, "What news?"

She then said, "I'm sorry; I apologize; I didn't mean to break any news to you, but you need to go find out what's going on."

I then ran home and waited for someone to tell me anything, but I was home with Papa, the cook and Mike (Micheal) the housekeeper, who did not have any information for me.

Hours had gone by, and I didn't hear anything from home. Communication was very difficult, and telephones were a big deal and reserved for those who could afford them. We had a phone, but I could not reach my dad. No cell phones; only land lines. It was evening, then night came; I still had not heard anything, so I went to bed, but I noticed a sadness came all over me, and as I slept I saw an image like my mother lying in a bed, lifeless, and then a chill came over me and I had a fever. I slept it off and awakened to the huge gates drawing back as my dad was driving in from Makurdi.

His face was firm, and I knew something was not right. I said hello to him, but he said, "How are you and why are you not in school?"

I told him, "I just woke up and I had a fever last night." Then I escorted him to the living area while Micheal and the driver unloaded the car. He sent the driver to campus to pick up my older sister Nancy. When Nancy arrived about an hour later, he broke the news to us that our mother had died in Saudi Arabia, and he was working tirelessly to bring her body back home, as it was not their custom to keep corpses. He said my mom had died about a month ago, but we were not informed, and he was not aware of it.

I was crushed; I could not breathe; my knees could not hold me, and I fell to the ground. My sister fell on top of me, and we wailed. My father cried also and walked into his room. The cook and the housekeeper helped us up, consoled us, and led us into the house.

From that day on, my life changed. That was my turning point; I lost interest in the very existence of life. I didn't want to eat, I didn't want to bathe, and I refused to go to school. Life became hopeless; my mother was my hero—I wanted to be in everything like her. I wrote her letters and she wrote letters back to me; I always went to the post office to receive mail from her; I looked forward to all her letters.

Life was useless. I had no one to turn to. My mother had taught me all that I knew about being a lady; she was intelligent and outgoing; everyone loved her; she added a sparkle everywhere she went.

It wasn't too long before all this emotion turned bad; I became very angry and wanted to get back at anything or anyone that I felt was the reason for her death, so I turned inward and blamed my father. "If only you didn't divorce her, she would not have left home." Then I blamed my step-mom. "If only you did not come into our home and break up our family." Then I blamed all my cousins and aunts who never talked my dad out of sending my mom away, and the list goes on. My social life was zero; I became an introvert and didn't have any interest in anyone except myself and didn't care much about what was going on around me.

A few weeks later, my father was able to bring my mother's corpse back home from Saudi Arabia. Everyone except me made it to her funeral, because my dad said I had to take an exam in school. To this day I do not know where my mother was buried, and I could not bring closure to her death. It made my grief so intense, I lost my joy and I almost became a robot. Everything was piling up emotionally, and I could not cope. So, I decided to quit college.

My father had come to Jos to visit us, and when it was time for him to leave, I packed my bags and told him I was not going back to school any more. I wanted to go back to Makurdi. He pleaded with me and asked why I was making this decision. I told him I just couldn't continue. I got my stuff, and that was the last time I was in Jos. School was done, and for five hours my dad and I drove in complete silence.

I came home, and I had only one day to breathe before my step-mother, Nyeru, rose up with vehemence and decided to make my life miserable all over again. It was like an ongoing misery. She was now comfortable that my mom would not be coming back to take what rightfully belonged to her. She came to my room to say, "Sorry about your mom," but I wasn't even looking at her.

My dad did not waste any time; in about a week I was registered into another university in my home town to study or at least obtain a Bachelor of Science in Accounting. My dad did not want any of his children to be without a basic education; he knew the value of education, and I am so thankful to my dad that he didn't give up on me. I was just a child locked up, looking for a way of expression in a society that was not ready for me. It was a constant battle between what I was created to be and do against what society and my father demanded of me. Back then, if you were an all-science student, which I was, it was a lot easier to switch to social sciences because you had the basic classes needed for the transition. I could not start the semester in the middle, so I had to wait until a new semester started.

My Uncle Joe, who lived in Lagos with his beautiful wife, Henrietta (we call her Aunty Hetty), thought it would be a clever idea for me to come out and visit with his family; his wife had just had a new baby. And it would give me an opportunity to leave the chaos at home.

My father did not object; he was willing to do anything to make sure I went to college. He saw how my mother's death was taking a toll on me, and if he didn't do something, my life would be in ruins.

We didn't have spiritual help; we didn't go to church or have any foundation; life just happened, if you know what I mean.

I was excited about going to Lagos. I had never left home to live in anyone's home before. My father was not in support of us visiting and staying with relatives; he always kept close eyes on us and paid us very close attention.

I was nineteen, and Lagos was about nine hours driving, so my dad decided to take me by plane, so we flew out to Lagos, and the next day he took me to my uncle's house. My dad left, and he told me to call him any time I was ready to come back home. That was not going to be long, in my mind.

My uncle's wife, Henrietta, was very welcoming and immediately loved me; she showed me around the house and the kitchen; she introduced me to her newborn son, Jessy, and I carried him while she cooked and cleaned. She spoke fluent French and worked with a French company. She always took me to work with her, and we stopped to buy ice cream, fried chicken and cakes on our way back home. Aunty Hetty was one of the best cooks I know. I noticed her house was peaceful, and she was very accommodating of everyone who came through, good or bad; then I realized they were a different type of Christian—they were born-again Christians and went to

101

church all the time. Aunty Hetty sang in the choir and my Uncle was the youth pastor heading the young discipleship (YDI) youth. It seemed pretty intense at the time.

After one week, my uncle said to me, "You are coming with us to church today."

I said, "But it's Wednesday."

He said, "Yes, it's a mid-week service; you will like it."

I said, "Okay."

When Wednesday came, we drove to Iyanaipaja where the church was located at the time, before moving to Shiloh. When we arrived, my uncle said, "This is Winners' Chapel Living Faith Church."

Then I said, "Okay," with a silly grin on my face. I was used to going into Catholic cathedrals with pews and bells and high ceilings and all of that, and before I could finish my thought, another car parked right beside ours, and a dark, slender man came out of the door with a white suit, and immediately everyone rushed to his side to usher him. Then I noticed when he saw my uncle, he stopped to say a word to him. At this time, I had stepped out of the car, and my uncle waved at me to come. And when I came closer to this man, I raised my head up, and his eyes were like fire; it pierced my soul. I quickly took my face away and then I heard my uncle say to him, Papa, this is my Niece; she came from Makurdi to spend some time with me, and she doesn't want to give her life to Christ; she keeps saying she is Catholic."

102

Papa lifted his hands and placed them on my head and prayed in English; he said, "Father, this is Your daughter," and then he prayed in a strange language; at the time I didn't understand he was praying in tongues, but he lifted up his hand, and when I looked back in his face again, he smiled and walked away.

I just stood there, I was in the presence of Bishop David Oyedepo and didn't know it. The church service was loud. People were rejoicing and dancing like they had no care in the world; they all screamed Halleluia in one accord and danced to the talking drums and spoke in strange voices. I kept my eyes opened all the time and I just observed what was going on. When we got home, my uncle asked me if I enjoyed the service, and I responded, "What was that all about?"

Not that day but several days later I started questioning in my heart, but never talked to anyone about it; I was so consumed with anger and resentment that I wasn't ready to let go. After two weeks, I was ready to go home; I enjoyed my vacation, but I was too used to my environment. I did call my dad, and he came and took me back to Makurdi.

It was time to start my new school in Benue State University. Even though I grew up in this part of the country, I didn't particularly care to go to college in the same state. I went to elementary and middle school, but all my school-age mates had left home and schooled out of state. I was a year behind, but at this point what did it matter?

I arrived at school—first day into the accounting department, and the Dean of Accounting was there to introduce us to accounting and what accounting was all about in ACC 101. I had this look on my face like, "Hurry up." By the time he was done with his last sentence, "Accounting is the basis of debit and credit...," I was in another world, more like in one of the many books I had read and wasn't paying attention. The next moment, someone was nudging me to introduce myself.

First day of class went well. I didn't know anyone and wasn't ready to make any friends, but two girls, who seemed to be the popular girls, came up to me and said, "Hello, do you want to come outside with us and eat Puff Puff and Coke?"

I said, "Sure, why not," and so we went under a tree where this lady had hot yeast dough frying in deep oil; we bought some, and there came Tweety Bird, full of life and chatty from the law department, but she always wanted to hang around the Accounting and Business Management students. Her name was Ari. I introduced myself to her, and from then on Jane, Ifynaya, Ari and I became friends. They lived on campus, but I came from home every day for the first semester and moved onto campus the following semester. Accounting was a great course and quite interesting, but it was not my forte, I didn't like the never-ending numbers, the statistical, analytical ways of answering simple questions; it all started getting boring. I was wired to be a care-giver, and I started dreading the possibility that I was going to be locked up in a corporate office environment one day crunching

104

numbers; it was unimaginable. We did what we had to do to pass our classes; we studied and crammed. We didn't have to like it, but we passed our exams and had a promise for a better life and future with education, at least that was what we were told.

Chapter 8: Meeting Paul, Getting Married; Paul's Death and Burial

Time went by fast, and I was in my third year. I was sitting with my friends Ari, Jane and Ify, when a car pulled up by the sidewalk and this six-foot-tall, dark-skinned man came out from his car, walked up to me and said, "Hello, Onyeje, how are you? I am Paul, and I went to the house to ask after you, and your dad told me you were on campus. Do you mind talking to me for a second?"

My friends started giggling and smiling; then I introduced them and said, "These are my friends Ari, Jane and Ify."

So, I got up and moved closer to his car and we started talking. I didn't know what it was, but I listened to what he had to say. He said he had heard about me and he wanted to see if I would be interested in going out with him some time to eat lunch or dinner, so we could talk. I said, "Okay," and when I went home, I told my dad that one named Paul came to see me in school and wanted us to go out sometime to eat. My dad told me that he looked like a good young man, but he was more interested in me completing school and not worrying about relationships right now.

At this point, I was not enjoying my home environment; my step-mom was making my life miserable, and I could never do anything right, so I came up with my own plan. If I got married, it looked good; I had a year to graduate from college and I could finally leave home and be free. That felt so good, and in my little twenty-one-year-old mind, it was perfect.

Paul was a trained pilot but could never fly a plane due to his poor vision, so he became the chief air traffic controller for the NAATC. He was good at what he did, and everyone liked him. He traveled a lot too and was involved in a national conference that took him to Japan, Taiwan and America. On several occasions he would love to have taken me with him, but my dad would never approve just because we had not been officially married, and my dad said it was not honorable to travel with a man I was not married to.

I had left school one time on a weekend to go see Paul in Abuja; that was the first time I had done something like that. I was afraid because I thought my dad would find out and that would be the end of me. I stayed with Paul over the weekend, and he brought me back to school.

By the end of that year, things had gotten serious, and he asked my dad if he could marry me. My dad said, "Okay. You have to talk to her. She has to complete her university or else she cannot come to live with you." He made a deal with my dad, and I said, "Yes." I was 22 years old and Paul was 35.

About a month later, I learned that I was pregnant, but I had no one to talk to. My mom was not around, but I was so afraid that my father would kill me if he found out, that I ran to Paul's sister who was a nurse doula, and she advised me to get rid of the pregnancy. She gave me some pills and asked me to swallow them. I was confused and told Paul that his sister asked me to take all these pills; he said it was up to me what I wanted to do. Because I was afraid, I took one of the three pills, and then I became very afraid.

That night as I slept, I had the weirdest dream; I heard crying babies in my dream, and I woke up in a sweat. I called my sisters Ebowo and Eneape. They encouraged me, covered my secret and told me it was going to be okay. I threw the remaining two pills in the trash and told Paul I wasn't going to do anything; what would happen to me would have to happen; I didn't care anymore.

It was December 13th, 1997, the day I would be married in the Catholic church in Makurdi. I was then 3 months pregnant, and as pale as a wall. I was not eating and was stressed out. Up until the day of the wedding, my father did not know I was pregnant. I had all the women around me dressing me up and preparing me for my wedding; my makeup was done, hair pulled up in a tight bun, and celebration was in the air, but a sadness was all around me that only I could feel; my heart was heavy; I missed my mom, as she was the only one at that moment I needed. I was so scared I didn't even know what I was about to do. I started to cry, and no one could console me.

The bells in the cathedral began to go off as everyone rose up and turned to the door. The cathedral door opened, and as I walked down the aisle, my little heart began to sink. I felt like I was fainting; my leg became like metal, like I was frozen, and then the organist played the song again as a cue for me to start marching. I walked down the aisle on my father's right hand; as he walked me down the aisle, I knew my life had changed forever.

My father placed my right hand in Paul's hands and stepped aside to stand beside his wife in the pews. Our vows were taken, and contracts were signed; several pictures were taken and the celebration continued until evening.

After the wedding, we drove back to our hotel suite, and I became so sick I didn't know whether I was going to make it. I spent the remaining two days in the hospital; that was when everyone found out I was pregnant. My father was upset, but it was too late now; I was married, so that made it better than nothing.

After the wedding, I had to go back to school to complete my last year in college. My father was not having it and had made Paul agree to allow me to complete my university education, so in my father's eyes nothing was official. I was heavily preganant and attending lectures on campus. I was not going for my usual antenatal care. I was 22 and didn't know any better.

In May of 1998, while I was walking from one class to the next, I felt a sharp pain in my abdomen. I was quickly taken home using public transportation, since there were no cell phones at the time. The pain got worse, and by the time six hours had passed, I was in so much pain I was pulling out my hair. My father was on a business trip, and

Paul had traveled out of the country. I was at home with my new stepmom. Why did I have a new stepmom? Let me explain.

Ten years had gone by since Nyeru and my dad got married. In Nigeria, the widespread belief is that women went to shrines and witch doctors to obtain black magic for marital purposes or for infertility to have children and some to have male children even after they have had multiple female children. It may not all be true, but what did we know as children at the time? We heard the older ones talking about it, that women who could not marry always went to the voodoo house to obtain black magic and cast a spell on the man they wanted. The spell didn't last but a few years, anywhere from five to ten years. It was not a secret. When Nyeru left our home abruptly, it was said in the street she had put a spell on my dad. Nyeru and my dad were inseparable, but they went from hot romance to worst enemies.

It was a rough ride those ten years. One evening my dad had called me to go into her room and see if she was there, because she wasn't answering him when he called for her. I ran up the stairs to her room and knocked on her door; when I didn't get an answer, I opened the door. I screamed, out of shock. Nyeru had left; her room was cleaned out; nothing was left. She was gone, and never came back. Nobody asked her to leave; she just got her stuff and left. I went back and told my dad what I had seen; he followed me to her room, but he turned around without saying a word, and walked away. I was happy she was gone for good.

110

My dad was without a wife for about three months. But by the time I was getting married, he had remarried another woman that was introduced to him by his older sister. Her name was Annie. She was stepmother number two.

By this time, my siblings and I were wiser and had gained some experience from our first step-mom; we knew what to do and what not to do. I was on my way out of the house, but I had thoughts of my siblings who still had to come back home. By this time my siblings hardly visited Makurdi; we all just wanted to stay out of trouble and strife. The new wife was younger than Nyeru; she had no formal education and could pass for one of our friends. She didn't know how to drive and didn't stay long enough to learn.

Back to my labor pains with my new stepmom. By the time I arrived home from school, the drivers had gone home for the day. My stepmom made me walk with her about a mile to an old midwife who was sitting under a mango tree drinking brukutu, a locally brewed drink of fermented millet with a high alcoholic content. She sat with a couple of her friends when we arrived; she then told me and my stepmother that I was in labor, and to put me on a bike and drive me to the women's center to have my baby. I made it to the clinic, and a bed was given to me where I laid screaming in pain. I didn't get any sympathy. All I was told was to be quiet, and that little girls don't get married or have babies. I was at the mercy of my stepmom and the drunk midwife. All my sisters were in school and no one was home. While the midwives were prepping me to have my baby, it started

111

pouring down rain and the electricity went out and everywhere was pitch dark. My stepmom had a little lantern in her hand while the drunk midwife with her dirty hands pulled the baby out of me. When the baby came out, I felt a relief, but there was an odd silence; the baby did not cry. Then I heard a whisper to bring the lamp closer—the baby had the umbilical cord wrapped around her neck and was choking to death. The midwife in her drunken state was able to think through the process. She turned my baby upside-down, pulled the cord over her head and jerked her twice with her legs. At this point I started to cry because I thought my baby was dead, and I said, "O God, please don't let my baby die." At that moment, I heard a loud cry. The cry of my baby was such a relief.

I was cleaned up and stitched up the best she could. I was then instructed on how to breast feed and hold the baby. I wasn't given anything to eat, but I was given a hot shower and a huge fabric band wrapped around my waist to keep my belly down. Everything was happening so fast, I wanted the day to break so I could leave and go back home.

It was a crude environment; even in my predicament I was able to observe that a lady came in to have her baby, and her baby did not make it; she was wailing, and no one consoled her. Another lady was having a baby beside me on the next bed. I didn't have the luxury of a private room, so there were three ladies cramped up in that room. As the lady kept pushing her baby out (she was having her fourth child), as soon as the baby was born—a baby girl—I remembered,

112

like yesterday, the lady hissing and saying, "Ooooo why another girl child? My husband will send me away from home!" Those words stayed with me till this day.

The following morning, our neighbor's wife heard I had had a baby, and she came to take me home. My dad came back from his business trip two days later and was so excited he had become a grandfather that he quickly bonded with Ihotu and started calling her Tutu. Paul was ecstatic too, when he got home about four days later.

A week after delivery, I discovered I had a massive infection from the non-sanitary way I had the baby, and the baby, unknown to me, had a broken leg from the jerking and pulling from my womb. It was hard to watch, when I pulled off Ihotu's diaper to change her, her leg would curl up to her chest like an elastic band; it was not a pretty sight. I woudn't allow anyone to see or touch her, so the doctors referred us to an orthopedic doctor in Enugu about three hours from Makurdi. While we prepared to make that journey, a very good friend had come to visit me at home; his name was Emmauel PoseE. He asked how I was doing, and I told him I was fine, but that Ihotu's right leg was broken and twisted, and we were referred to an orthopedic doctor in Enugu. Then, looking intently at me, he said, "Can I pray for her leg, because God will heal her."

I said, "Okay, that's fine." I didn't quite understand anything about that at the time, but I was willing to accept anything that would help my baby. He prayed for her leg to be healed, and after he left, the next day while I was bathing my baby, I realized her right leg did not spring back to her chest and was perfectly fine. I was so excited, and it has been that way ever since. We didn't have to go to Enugu to see the orthopedic doctor!

To make up for the time Paul was away when I had our baby, he decided a Christmas vacation to New York would help. At the time, I was one semester away from graduating with an accounting degree at the Benue State University. I was writing my final project on "money market and the economy," so a trip to the New York Stock Exchange sounded like a clever idea. We got ready and Paul obtained our visas and passports from the embassy. We flew out from Lagos the first week in December and arrived at JFK International Airport twelve hours later. I remember looking through the window so many thousands of feet in the sky, and when I did see the Statue of Liberty, something leaped in my heart, and I fell in love with America. It was a beautiful sight from up there; there was snow all over the place; I had never seen snow before, only in the movies, and I was in awe; it was going to be a white Christmas. I was so excited, I clutched Paul's hands, and he said, "Baby, I know you will love America."

We arrived safely, retrieved all our luggage and hailed a taxi to Paul's sister, who lived in a high-rise apartment in Queens. Paul had traveled a lot and was pretty used to the style. I was exhausted and had a nursing baby. His sister, Omada, welcomed us, and for the next three weeks that was going to be our home.

The next morning, Paul was up early and was ready to hit the streets of New York. We went to McDonalds; I didn't particularly care for the taste of the food. I just didn't taste it; I wasn't used to eating a burger that early. We hailed a taxi and went downtown. We walked back and forth in the streets. The buildings were intriguing—all the skyscrapers and fancy stores, designers and what have you; I wanted to go into all the stores. We shopped and shopped and shopped even on the streets as well. The next day we repeated the same thing.

By the third day we made it to the New York Stock Exchange building. This was in December of 1998; it was very easy to freely go in and out of the stock exchange building with no questions asked. It was interesting to see how the men on the floor did their trading; as an accounting student it gave me a better understanding of what to expect in the business world. I did see stocks going back and forth; the men had to walk away to the sidewalk to smoke a cigarette to ease the stress. It was a very high-tension environment, but very interesting to watch. I did take notes and asked a few questions, and back on the streets we went.

It was freezing cold in New York and I hated the weather. By the second week, we had made it to the other side of Manhattan and wanted to go to Staten Island, but missed the ferry, so we decided to come back another day, but we never did.

On Sunday morning, we attended mass at a Catholic church in Queens, attended by the priest, his altar boys, ten senior citizens, Paul, his sister, me and little Tutu. That was the coldest environment! No one spoke to us, and we did not speak to anyone. We sang from a hymnal, and the altar boys walked in slow motion around the altar with incense. I was careful not to laugh as is my manner when I get nervous.

Paul's sister, Omada, was a devout Catholic and counted her rosary beads every night. The only time she placed the rosary down was when she got on the phone at four a.m. to gossip. I guess the rosary beads were not needed for that conversation. I was tiptoeing to the bathroom one night because the studio was so small, and I didn't want to wake anyone up. When I took two steps, I noticed Omada's door was slightly cracked, and she was sobbing over the phone. She had made an international call to her sister Joyce in Nigeria. She was making sure they knew that the wife Paul had married had high tastes, and her brother was not going to be able to maintain her. She said the marriage was too early for Paul to have traveled with me all the way to America to expose me to the fancy life. She said she had been very sick, and since Paul arrived with his wife, she had not had any sleep, and the baby kept crying all night. She said, "Paul's wife makes me wait on her, and can't cook," and she went on and on.

I almost walked into her room and choked her with the rosary beads! At twenty-three years old I was too naïve to understand why a woman of over forty at the time would do such a thing. The next morning, she came in and smiled, then said, "I hope you all had a good night; I slept

116

well, and I was wondering if you all would like to go to JC Penney today."

Paul said, "Sure, why not?"

And I said, "No thank you." Then I turned to Paul, winked at him and said we needed to talk.

Omada had a little white companion who came to run errands for her; his wife was stuck in a nursing home somewhere, so he had come to pick Omada up for some grocery shopping, because she never drove or owned a car. She was very afraid and terrified even of her shadow; she constantly looked over her shoulders when we were in public and had a bedroom filled with boxes of clothes and junk up to the ceiling. I think she was a hoarder because she slept on the couch to make room to collect her stuff. She never walked out the door without her six layers of makeup and would turn her guests out if she was not notified hours before they came. She made Paul go downstairs one day to see a friend who came to see him. Now I understand what I didn't know then, that she was on so many medications and probably was losing her mind.

She had been in America for twenty-three years at the time we visited and had never been back to Nigeria. She came at the age of 18; I really don't know the back story. Anyway, as she went out with Mr. Laudary, I did tell Paul all she had said the night before. Paul was cross but mature about it, so when she came back home later that evening, Paul thanked her for her hospitality, called the airlines and

117

changed our flight schedule. We packed our luggage to come back home. We had spent two weeks and a few days, and it was time for me to resume school. My dad had already started calling and wanted me to come back home.

We arrived back home in Nigeria safe and sound and boarded a flight from Lagos to Abuja. When we arrived back home in twenty-four hours, Pauline, Paul's older sister, arrived at our home. I said, "Hello, aunty."

She didn't respond. She walked past me going straight to our bedroom and calling out "Paul, Paul, Paul." When Paul got out of the shower, she was sitting on the bed and said, "I came to pick up all the stuff Omada sent you to bring for me from America."

Pauline's manner was to walk into our home and walk into our bedroom; it did not matter what time of the day it was. At this point, I still did not know what I was up against. I was brought up in a home where at twenty-three years old, I didn't have many of the worldly-wise ways of dealing with inlaws, dealing with men or having a family. I didn't know what it entailed; I was just living my life. But fear was beginning to creep in. I had no defense. I wasn't able to tell anyone what Pauline was doing; I thought that was how it was supposed to be.

Paul asked her to go downstairs and wait for him to get dressed, and then he apologized to me for her behavior. Pauline was a lawyer and a very strong-willed woman. Pauline got what she wanted from

118

whomever she wanted and was never apologetic about it; everyone in the family was afraid of her, and she beat up her husband one time because the girls were loving on him. He was a fine young doctor who was good at what he did, but we had him at our home two times every week, running away from Pauline. She whooped him really good for conduct. I always laughed and told myself, *"How can a big man like this be beat up by a short woman?"* I guess she had her techniques or a different weapon of warfare—wooden spoon, hot water, knives, who knows—it's Nigeria; no laws against domestic violence, at least none that I knew of at the time. I always excused myself when he arrived; I was only one year into my marriage, and the drama was overwhelming. Paul settled every family situation, but it kept mounting. He made sure all his nieces and nephews got return flights back to college after the holidays; every one of his family wanted a piece of Paul.

Pauline finally got all the stuff that was sent to her by Omada and wanted to know all that Paul had purchased, so I brought everything out one after the other and showed each piece to her. I was only twenty-three; what did I know? I forgot I was in a Nigerian cultural marriage; no one told me how to do it.

In May of 1999, a week before Paul's 36th birthday, we were taking a walk and having very long conversations about life and about baby Tutu, and he told me he was sorry; he did not deserve me, but that I was just an innocent girl who needed to grow up in life. He said that when he saw me, all he wanted was for me to be his wife, and nothing

119

was going to stop him from having me. He said he should not have pushed.

I didn't know where he was going with the conversation, but I kept teasing, and he stopped talking and said, "Baby, I am traveling tomorrow to Yankari Game Reserve; would you like to come? It is in Bauchi state and only 3 hours from Abuja. Then I'll take you back to school and wait for my suspension to be over before going back to work."

Paul had huge ambitions; he was in his third year of law school while working as an air traffic controller; he was suspended because the terminal where he worked at the airport had no air conditioner. It had broken down and they had to work in that hot sticky glass building. He had complained and notified his boss, but nothing was done to fix it. Unfortunately for him, the President of Nigeria, Olusegun Obasanjo, at the time was flying into the country, and as the presidential plane approached the airport, the air traffic controller was nowhere to be found; they called Paul and he refused to answer, so they found someone else who helped the president's pilot land safely. Paul was given a query and suspended without pay.

On the night before the Yankari trip, Paul's older brother called and told him he had a business trip in Bauchi and asked if it was okay to travel with him. Paul did not ask me if it was okay. By morning, his older brother arrived, and stuffed his luggage into the trunk of the car. Then I told Paul that his older brother was here and had stuffed his

120

luggage into the trunk; was he aware that we were traveling to Yankari Game Reserve as a family? He said, "Oh Baby, I am sorry I forgot to tell you, but he is coming with us; he needs to get some business taken care of in Bauchi."

I said "Okay," but I wasn't happy about it; I did not show that I was upset.

His brother walked around to the front of the car and sat down. Then Paul opened the door to the back of the vehicle for Tutu and me. At that moment I could not take it any more. I felt humiliated and disrespected. I turned around and told Paul, "I think it would be better if you and your brother go to Bauchi and take care of business; we can go to the game reserve another time."

Paul did not want to show his brother that I disapproved of his traveling with us, so he got into the car and said, "Baby, I'll call you when I arrive." He closed the door and drove off. While he drove off, I stood outside of the front door; it felt like I could not move. I didn't understand a thing spiritually, but it looked like I saw a ball of fire behind them.

I walked into the house and up the stairs into our bedroom. I laid Tutu down on the bed. I opened our closet and took Paul's white agbada robe and put it over my head and was playing in front of the mirror with Tutu. After a while I took it off and laid beside Tutu on the bed and we both fell asleep. That was about 10:30 a.m.

We both fell into a deep sleep and didn't wake up again until I heard a loud knock on the door. I ran downstairs to open the door, but everywhere was dark, so I turned on the light. It was now a little dark outside at 6:30 p.m. Tutu and I had slept for close to 8 hours. Then I realized I had not heard from Paul; he should have called four hours ago. I reached out and opened the door, and the man standing outside said, Madam, are you Mrs. Ofikwu?"

I said, "Yes, how can I help you?"

He said, "Can I come in?"

I said, "Yes."

He said, "Is Paul Ofikwu at home?"

I said, "No, he went to Bauchi this morning with his brother, and he was supposed to call me when he arrived, but I haven't heard from him; I was sleeping and maybe the phone rang, and I didn't hear it."

When I said that, I noticed the man's face dropped to the floor, and he said, "Okay, thank you. I am one of his colleagues, and I just wanted to know if he was home." He turned around and left.

In thirty munutes, Pauline arrived, and straightway walked into the house and asked me, "Where is your husband, Paul?"

I said, "He went to Bauchi this morning and hasn't called me since."

She said, "Okay," and then she started pulling off the chair covers of the chairs; they were beautiful chair backs I had bought while I was in New York, and I remembered Pauline had asked me if she could have them, and I told her I wanted to use them for my living room.

I looked at her and said, "Aunty, why are you pulling off my chair covers? And what is going on?" But she kept pulling the chair covers off and said nothing.

It wasn't long, perhaps an hour after Pauline had left that my older sister, Nancy, arrived. She was working in Abuja at the time, and she said she wanted to come by and check on me and Tutu to make sure we were doing okay. That was when I knew something was wrong, but I didn't know what, and I never in my imagination thought anything could have happened to Paul. I thought maybe he was upset with me that I did not follow him to Bauchi, so he didn't want to call me. My big sis said she didn't think anything was wrong, but I could tell she was uncomfortable and was very quiet.

She slept over that night and in the morning another of Paul's sisters, Christy, sent her driver to take me and Ihotu to her house in Maitama in Abuja. She was a sweet lady and was very close to Paul. When we arrived, she was her cheerful self and she said, "We are going to go to Makurdi. I need you to eat, and we'll be on our way." I told her I wasn't hungry; inside of me I wanted to scream, "Can someone tell me what is going on?"

The car got loaded and we headed for Makurdi. One hour into the journey, I noticed Tutu had stood up on my lap in the car. She was only eleven months old. She turned backward, facing the rear side and waving to an anonymous person, and she kept smiling and waving and giggling, but when I turned back to look through the back window, all I saw was dust. After this incident my heart began to race; I knew something terrible had happened.

None of my family members were present; I was in the car with Christy and her driver. We arrived at Makurdi shortly before it got dark. I was taken to Paul's oldest sister, the first daughter of the Ofikwu family, where the house was packed with people. My father was not present, my stepmother was not there, so no one had informed my dad what was happening; my father was on a business trip. Later I was told my older sister called my dad, and he was on his way back from his trip. But I was among my in-laws, people that I had only known for less than two years, and some I had never met. I dropped my bag and sat down. I had not been offered a cup of water but had traveled for five hours. I noticed Paul's older sister rushing toward me and the other ladies were trying to hold her back, but she was too quick for them. She was face-to-face with me and our noses were almost touching, and with no sympathy in her eyes she said to me in my traditional Idoma dialect, "**Your husband Paul had an accident, and he is dead.**"

So many of you reading this book may never have heard about the West African traditions or cultures surrounding the death of a spouse.

124

Most of the practices are generally barbaric across the board with very few differences; I will try to elaborate as much as I can to give you a clear understanding. Someday I pray that the barbaric and inhuman practices of widows in West Africa and Africa in general will come to a stop. The Igbos, Yoruba and Hausas have very similar practices; the other tribes and ethnic groups practice what their forefathers had passed down from one generation to the next. The death of a spouse is a painful experience and enough to shatter a person's life forever. The widows are treated with disrespect and dishonor from the day her husband dies; she is subjected to cruel treatment, harrassment and dejection from the very family that once took her as a beautiful bride.

I will share the Igbo traditional widowhood practice although I am not Igbo. My village Otukpa and Paul's village were not so far from the Igbos' land where some of the cultural practices are very similar. I spent my time researching a lot of the practices and cultures, and I found so many different experiences and practices, all cannot be documented in this book. But some can.

In some parts of Igbo land, when a man dies, the wife will tie a wrapper over her chest without a blouse. She must not talk to anyone and will not have a bath until her husband is buried. After the burial, the "Umuada" (daughters of the man's ancestors) will come to shave her hair, bathe her in an open compound, only having the privacy of being surrounded by the "Umuada," oblivious of the tragic loss which every widow suffers due to the death of their husbands. Callous in-laws conspire to apply vicious burial rites to dehumanize the

125

embattled widow. They confront her with questions on how and when the deceased husband died, the circumstance that led to his death, what she did to save him from dying, and her extent of contact with the late husband's family before his death. The explanations are never satisfactory. The widow must drink the water used in bathing the corpse of her husband to prove her innocence. There is no end to the humiliating punishment encountered by widows under the cover of native laws and traditions.

Among the Igbo people of Nigeria, the relatives demand a document relating to the deceased's properties including lands, investments and bank accounts, and the widows were required to take oaths as proof that the knowledge of relevant land and personal property of the deceased were not concealed. Subsequently, the widows were required to provide expensive items like a white goat and two jars of palm wine for purification purposes to the female members of their husband's lineage who made and implemented decisions on every matter concerning widows. The widows were forbidden to touch any object including themselves without defilement. Hence, they were given pieces of sticks to scratch their bodies, while their food was also cooked in old pots rather than those normally used for cooking for other members of the family. Also, they were to sleep on old mats placed on wooden planks which would be burnt at the end of the mourning period. If a woman dies during the one-year mourning period, she is perceived as being responsible for her husband's death and therefore commits an abomination. Hopefully the widow was not

126

sassy and outspoken during the time she was married, then it will be payback time.[1]

Generally, most of these harmful widowhood practices include: shaving of hair, wearing of black/white clothes, sleeping on the floor or mat, refraining from taking a bath for a period of time, being made to swear with husband's corpse, and seclusion. All of these barbaric practices are meant to make the widow unattractive and to present herself to everyone that her husband is dead; she sleeps on the floor as a symbol of her dethronement from being a wife and a part of the family; not taking her bath or personal hygiene is to show her love for her late husband. Most of these women bear it because they believe it is the right thing to do.[2] By the time you have finished this mourning period, you are so messed up emotionally you are covered with shame and guilt and have no self-worth or value.

With Christianity and modernization, some of these practices are changing, but the dark side of these practices is upheld in most parts, and the widows suffer silently.

As Paul's sister was still speaking, another of her sisters came to pull her away from me. I collapsed, and the next time I woke up, someone was fanning me. I had fainted, and I started bleeding like I was having another period. I could not cry, I could not scream, and my world just stopped; it looked like the carpet under my feet was being pulled away. I could not call on God; I didn't know Him yet. I had no mother to hold on to, no family to cry with; I wailed among strangers for two days before my family arrived; I was on the floor crying for two days. I could not eat, and I could not sleep. I remember Cecilia the nurse, one of Paul's sisters, came by and gave me Valium because it was going on 48 hours and I had not had any sleep. I did take the medication, but it was of no use. I was going through some emotions that words could not describe. I felt heat and cold go down my spine all at the same time; my abdomen was shot and I was suffocating.

Pauline all the while had been looking for the right opportunity to talk to me, and I noticed she had been making her circles around me. She finally got close enough to my ears and whispered, "Your husband told me he bought you a Jetta car for your graduation; it was a surprise so he didn't want you to know about it. He parked the car at his friend's house. So do you know where the key to the car is?"

Those words burned down my veins like hot oil; I could not believe what I was hearing. Paul's body had not even been released back to Makurdi from Bauchi. It was day four. I looked directly at Pauline and stared right into her eyes and I told her, "I don't know what you're talking about."

She said, "Okay, we shall see," and got up and went back to the kitchen area where all the other sisters were hanging out.

Paul died a painful death, and I would never wish it on anyone. The morning he left for Bauchi, it was one of those seasons in Nigeria with a gruesome fuel scarcity. Most people had to carry their own fuel in a container in the car when traveling because you never knew if you

128

would find fuel to purchase. Paul had about a 50-liter Jerrycan in his trunk, and as he approached the city, he had an accident trying to avoid an oncoming vehicle and struck a neaby tree. Immediately the car caught on fire. Paul got out of the car as fast as he could, but then he heard his brother's voice calling him back because he was trapped. So, Paul ran back to the slightly burning car, pulled his brother out and threw him away from the car onto the main road. He didn't turn fast enough, and the fire had reached the trunk of the car and the fuel in the car exploded, and Paul was engulfed in the ball of fire. He did not drop and roll; he ran back and forth, and the fire got bigger and bigger until he fell on his knees, melted, and burned to ashes, with his older brother and people watching him. No emergency services, no 911, nothing. Till this day I cannot imagine what pain he felt in those last moments. What was he saying? Did he call out for me and Tutu? Did he call out to God?

I was told he was crying and screaming for help as his brother recapped. That was my husband, that was the father of my daughter; why did he have to die that way? Why did he go back to the vehicle; couldn't his brother have pulled himself out of the car? Don't judge me; these are raw emotions and thoughts that I had to live with for so many years to come. At that moment all these emotions and questions were going through my mind. I could not voice them to anyone because I thought that would have been a wicked question to ask. I bottled a lot of things in my heart and it was gradually eating me away. After the fire was put out by the villagers, it was too late. Paul's older brother was taken to the hospital for minor scratches and stage-two burns on his arms. But Paul did not survive; his body was then identified by his brother and prepared to be sent home.

My dad was not informed that Paul had passed away; he was on a business trip and, finally on the 3rd day, someone got a hold of him and told him what had happened. He immediately came back home. I was not in our family house; I was with the Ofikwus, and no one from my family had arrived until the third day because they were not told. I was crying among strangers, I was scared, and had no one to hold on to. But when I lifted up my eyes and saw my dad walk through the door, he reached out to me and held my hands and consoled me. He didn't say much as was his nature, but when I looked into his eyes, I knew he was very disturbed and concerned. He took off his hat and held it to his chest, and with his right hand he held my hands. I didn't see a tear, but his eyes were red, and I knew he was weeping on the inside.

I am forever grateful that my dad stood by me; he wanted to protect me the best he could. He understood the traditions and the journey ahead in preparation for Paul's burial. He was a strong man and very principled; he was liked by many and commanded the respect of those around him.

My sisters, one after the other, left all they were doing and came to be with me; none of my sisters or family knew I was traveling to Makurdi. I did not know what was happening either. Ofu was in Jos at the time and had a vision, as he told me about later. He said at night he was asleep, and that Paul came to him and said, "Everyone is in Makurdi; what are you doing in Jos?" It was then that he got a taxi and came back to Makurdi and found out that uncle P. had died. (All my siblings called him uncle P.)

I was breast-feeding my baby at the time, and I stopped abruptly because of all that had happened. I was in so much pain I could not express my milk or tell anyone I was in so much pain. I had no privacy, and at least 8 to 9 people sat around me all day everyday; it was suffocating. When my sisters came, they took Tutu, and I didn't have to worry about her; I could not continue breast-feeding her. And that was how she was weaned.

Gradually, as the news spread, more people started coming, to see who Paul's wife was and what she looked like. Some came to sympathize with me, others pointed accusing fingers at me. In the traditional African culture, if a young man dies, something or someone has to take the blame for it. I was too young to understand the situation I was in. My life had just changed in front of me; I was now labeled a widow. The beloved young wife became the hated one; not too long afterwards, the whispering started. By day six, I was too weak to even cry or eat. I couldn't sleep, and I just sat down on the floor waiting for my next instruction.

One lady had come up to me and said, "Young lady, why have you stopped crying? It's been only 6 days, and it looks like your eyes are bright. You know everyone is looking at you; this is not the time to look pretty." She sat herself down in a chair and rolled over and fell on me and started screaming, "Ooooo, Paul our son is dead; how could you have done this to our wife? Oooooo, Paul, you can't just leave this world unannounced, leaving your wife and daughter. Ooooooo, Paul, Paul, our beloved son." She kept on with the eulogy, and as she screamed and wailed, a bunch of women joined in; no words could describe the emotions in that room. The air was thick with grief; you could almost touch it with your fingers.

After about an hour, another lady walked into the room and asked everyone to stop crying and get ready for lunch. At the time, I didn't know professional mourners existed, or that it was a thing anyone would love to do. I later found out that professional mourners move from one funeral ground to the next, stirring up emotions and crying; then they eat and leave and come back the next day to do it all over again.

On the 7th day, Paul's corpse had arrived, and the convoy was ready to drive to his village for burial. The Idoma tradition was very similer to the Igbo tradition when it came to marriage and burial. The family wanted Tutu and I to sit in the car that had the coffin, but my dad stepped in to say, "No, my daughter will ride with me in a different vehicle; she has been through enough trauma, and she will not be able to take the four-hour-long drive sitting and glancing at her husband's coffin. I will make sure I drive as close as possible." So Tutu and I rode in the same car with my dad and the driver. My dad had made special arrangements for a bus to go to my university campus to pick up some of my classmates who wanted to go to the funeral and support me. Paul's co-workers came with a few of his friends and family. My brothers and sister came, except for the the very young ones. It was very encouraging to see my classmates.

The drive to Paul's village was long, even though it was only four hours; it felt like twelve. No one could encourage me to eat, but I remembered drinking a little water when I was thirsty. I was not hungry, I did sleep all through the drive, and my dad did not say a word all through the journey. As we arrived, it was before dusk, and my dad woke me up and said, "We have arrived. I want you to remain strong. This is not going to be easy, but I will protect you. All your aunties arrived earlier from Otukpa (my father's village) this morning, and they will keep you with them. Always stay with them. Tutu is taken care of; your sisters have her with them."

The grave had been prepared a few days ahead; because of the nature of his death, the body could not stay for any protocol. My dad pleaded with the elders of the village and told them that I was too young, and he didn't want me to have the image of Paul in this state, so he would prefer if I didn't see his burnt corpse. Permission was granted, so I was led to the room where my aunties were all sitting, waiting for me. All seven of my aunties were precious to me: Mama Mary, my father's immediate older sister; Mama Original; Mama Eneape; Mama Rose; my name sake, Mama Onyeje; Mama Alami, my mother's only sister; and Mama Ebenyi. Sad to say that all those strong women have passed on except Mama Rose and Mama Original and never lived to read this story; they all died within four to seven years of this incident.

As I sat among my aunties, they made a circle around me and did not allow anyone to touch me. A lady walked into the room and demanded my wedding ring; my aunties asked her why she wanted the wedding ring. The lady said, "They need it at the burial ground to place inside the coffin; also we want to use it to swear by Paul that his wife is innocent. If after this is done and she is alive after seven days, then we'll know that she is innocent."

When I heard that, my heart broke into different pieces; I began to feel pain that was out of this world. I could not believe what I just heard. I couldn't even imagine someone would think of something so evil. I needed my mom, but she was nowhere close. I didn't have any relationship with God, so I could not call on Him. The pain was intense, and the void was getting deeper. At that moment my aunty said, "Sorry, we can't allow you to have her wedding band; we have to talk to her father about it."

The lady said, "Unfortunately we can't wait, because the funeral is about to take place and we don't have time to go back and forth. This is our tradion and we have to follow the rules."

It was getting dark, and there was no electricity. I noticed the compound was empty; all the men had gone to the graveside, and as the conversation was going on, my mind was racing, not knowing what would happen. I took my left hand and placed it under my thigh and sat on it. I was not going to let go of my ring; something on the inside of me did not feel right about it. I heard a loud gunshot, not one, but seven shots fired, and then silence. Paul had been buried. The woman said, "Well I guess you can prove your innocence later," and she spoke loud enough for everyone to hear as she started to walk away from us. She added, "Most of these young girls in university when they marry have boyfriends in school, and the spirit of Aleku (a god) always kills the innocent husband." She walked off, and as I began to cry, my aunties encouraged me and asked me not to pay attention to what had just been said.

About half an hour later, everyone who had gone to the graveside started walking back, and the compound started getting full again. People were heard crying a mile away, and as women rushed into the room, some tried to touch me and pull at me; others said, "We want to see Paul's wife. She has never been to Ondo (Paul's village) before. Bring her out so we can see her." My aunties kept their hands off and would not allow anyone to touch me. I bet my aunties understood something I didn't.

By 7 p.m., the in-laws had fed everyone who came; people sat outside under the moonlight and drank palm wine and ate. That was what a typical traditional burial looked like. This type of practice could go on for three to five days, depending on how buoyant the family was.

Now, while they did protect me, there was a traditional rite I had to perform; they would not be able to go with me for this. In the dark, I was taken to the back of the house, stripped naked and ordered to squat; a bucket of what I thought was water was set before me, and the ladies bathed me with the water. It was dirty water and didn't smell good; it was some type of ritual bath for the widow. It was cold and dark. I knew if I survived this time of my life, I was good. The same clothes I had on for a week were put back on me, and I was orderd to go back into the room.

First thing in the morning, I was approached by another lady who said, "Today is the day we have to shave your hair."

I was in shock and I was cooperative; nothing meant anything to me, but my dad walked up to the lady and said, "I'll pay the fine for not shaving her hair here; when I take her back to Otukpa, her mother's sister will shave her hair." They agreed on a price and my father went ahead and gave some money for my hair.

My dad was a no-nonsense man; he then said to my in-laws, "It is unfortunate what has happened. No one can change the situation, but we can make it better gradually. I beg of you all and ask for your permission to take my daughter from here to my village for a week and then back to Makurdi. She is in school and will have to take time to adjust back to her new life. This is not easy on anyone especially since she is so young."

136

Permission was granted, and we left Paul's village to go to Otukpa, about an hour-and-a-half drive. When we arrived, my father's compound was full of well wishers and mourners, and it was nonstop for another 3 days. My aunty Alami took me into my room and, with her hand armed with a pack of tiger razor blades, she shaved all my hair off. As my locks fell to the ground, I started to cry. The pain of my loss was unbearable, and from that day on, I wanted my life to end. I just could not take it any more. I remembered the first shower I had after that, when the water touched my scalp it burned because the blade had nicked my scalp in so many different places. I would not look at myself in a mirror; I covered all the mirrors in my room with fabric. I felt ugly, guilty, and ashamed. I was hurt beyond words could ever describe, and then I was angry at life itself and angry at myself; I felt like I had failed myself, and although I was thin, I was carrying 300 lbs. of sorrow and shame and regret everywhere I went.

Now reality was gradually dawning. Everyone had gone back to their homes; it was time for me to leave Otukpa and go back to Makurdi. As we arrived in Makurdi, I could not go back to school just yet; my emotions were raw, so I stayed home all semester, 3 months total. In those three months, I didn't go out in public. I stayed home and sat in my room most of the time. Some days, my schoolmates would come by the house to say hello, but a lot of them had moved on; they had to live their lives and had only three months to graduate. I was getting bored with nothing to do.

A special thanks to Nwanegbo, N. A, & Nzewi, D. for the contributions in the article I referenced about widowhood practices in some Nigerian societies. A retrospective examination.

PART II: MY JOURNEY
Chapter 9: Meeting Veronica Enewa Aluma

One afternoon while I was in my room, depressed and crying, Tutu was outside playing in the compound. Then I heard a knock on the door; I answered and asked whoever was outside to come in. I usually will leave my hair to air, but when I heard the knock at the door, I quickly picked up my scarf and wrapped it around my hair.

My mourning garments were not black; the local tailor had made me two long, white, long-sleeved robes with enough space around the neck to fit my head and small side slits so I could walk. I switched them out every other day to wash and dry, and for the next 6 months that was all I had to wear; nothing less was expected; I was being watched by everyone; it didn't really matter to me; I was not concerned about it anyway, I was just hurt.

And as my door opened, this lady walked into my room; she was about 38 or 39 at the time. She sat down beside me on the sofa in my room, and with the softest voice she said, "Are you Onyeje?"

I replied, "Yes, ma."

She said, "My name is Veronica Aluma, and I am the founder of House of Mercy." She then said, "God has come to give you life and life more abundantly. I heard about what happened to you, and I have come to see you." She talked with me for awhile and told me her story and how God had brought her through.

By the time she was done talking to me, she asked me if I wanted to give my life to Christ. I said, "Yes," and she held my hands and prayed the prayer of salvation with me. When I said "Amen," instantly I felt a load lifting off my shoulder; it felt like I could breathe again. I took a deep breath and started to cry.

She said, "You're now born again; you are a child of God." She spoke words into my life and commanded me to take off the grave clothes. She asked me to come to church whenever I could, and if I would get into trouble, I could come to church when my father was not home.

She asked me if I had a Bible, and I told her we had a Good News Bible lying around somewhere that we used in school for Christian religious study. She asked me to read Isaiah 54 and then, when I could, to purchase another Bible.

When she left, I picked up the Bible and quickly turned to the chapter she indicated, and as I read those words, my eyes got big, and hot tears flowed even more. Something was happening to me; the more I read, the more I cried. It said in Isaiah 54:1–17 KJV:

> *1 Sing, O barren, thou that didst not bear; break forth
> into singing, and cry aloud, thou that didst not travail
> with child: for more are the children of the desolate
> than the children of the married wife, saith the Lord.*

140

2 Enlarge the place of thy tent, and let them stretch forth the curtains of thine habitations: spare not, lengthen thy cords, and strengthen thy stakes;

3 For thou shalt break forth on the right hand and on the left; and thy seed shall inherit the Gentiles, and make the desolate cities to be inhabited.

4 Fear not; for thou shalt not be ashamed: neither be thou confounded; for thou shalt not be put to shame: for thou shalt forget the shame of thy youth, and shalt not remember the reproach of thy widowhood any more.

5 For thy Maker is thine husband; the Lord of hosts is his name; and thy Redeemer the Holy One of Israel; The God of the whole earth shall he be called.

6 For the Lord hath called thee as a woman forsaken and grieved in spirit, and a wife of youth, when thou wast refused, saith thy God.

7 For a small moment have I forsaken thee; but with great mercies will I gather thee.

8 In a little wrath I hid my face from thee for a moment; but with everlasting kindness will I have mercy on thee, saith the Lord thy Redeemer.

9 For this is as the waters of Noah unto me: for as I have sworn that the waters of Noah should no more go over the earth; so have I sworn that I would not be wroth with thee, nor rebuke thee.

10 For the mountains shall depart, and the hills be removed; but my kindness shall not depart from thee, neither shall the covenant of my peace be removed, saith the Lord that hath mercy on thee.

11 O thou afflicted, tossed with tempest, and not comforted, behold, I will lay thy stones with fair colours, and lay thy foundations with sapphires.

12 And I will make thy windows of agates, and thy gates of carbuncles, and all thy borders of pleasant stones.

13 And all thy children shall be taught of the Lord; and great shall be the peace of thy children.

14 In righteousness shalt thou be established: thou shalt be far from oppression; for thou shalt not fear: and from terror; for it shall not come near thee.

15 Behold, they shall surely gather together, but not by me: whosoever shall gather together against thee shall fall for thy sake.

16 Behold, I have created the smith that bloweth the coals in the fire, and that bringeth forth an instrument for his work; and I have created the waster to destroy.

17 No weapon that is formed against thee shall prosper; and every tongue that shall rise against thee in judgment thou shalt condemn. This is the heritage of the servants of the Lord, and their righteousness is of me, saith the Lord.

Wow! I read this passage every morning, in the afternoon and at night. I held on to every word and it was becoming personal. I didn't know how to pray or talk to God, so I just read those verses out loud to myself and back to God.

Six months had finally gone by and I was going into the seventh month. I had stayed home and not done anything new. I started to slowly try to leave my room during the day and walk around our compound and talk to a few people working around the house. I had not ventured into the market yet or walked on the street close to the house or entered any public gathering.

On this weekday, my father had gone on a business trip and would not be back for a couple of days. I had taken off my mourning gown and put on some regular clothes, so I would be inconspicuous. I walked about a half a mile to the next street and hailed an okada. I clutched my Bible and my handbag as I sat on the back side of the motor bike. I was so afraid; I didn't want to be recognized by anyone.

I left Tutu at home most of the time where our people could take care of her.

The okada driver asked me where I was going, and I replied, "North Bank to House of Mercy."

But then he said, "It will be better if you used a regular bus because it's a fifteen-minute ride and across the bridge over the river Benue."

I hopped down and waited on the road a few more minutes and then I flagged down a mini-bus going in that direction. I hopped into the bus, and it felt so different being out in public again. I enjoyed the new freedom I was experiencing, but fear gripped my heart because I didn't know the consequences of my actions. As I sat in the mini-bus, I noticed a bunch of women in the bus who had Bibles and were conversing about the House of Mercy, so I listened and waited to follow them to where they where going. I had never been to this place before. I didn't know what to expect, so I looked through the window into the vast waterbed across river Benue. It was so beautiful then. I felt warm tears rolling down my cheeks; I was lost in thought.

As the bus stopped and everyone emptied out, I mustered enough courage to ask one of the ladies getting out of the bus, "Where are you going, because I'm going to the House of Mercy."

She said, "Oh, you mean Abundant Life Sisters Fellowship?"

I said, "I don't know, but I am going to House of Mercy, and Mommy Aluma asked me to come."

144

The lady said, "O come; let's go. This is the right stop."

I paid the conductor of the bus (that was what they were called) and hopped right out. As we approached the building, I noticed more people were coming, mostly women: young women, teenagers, older women; and it didn't take long before the building was filled with women—over three hundred.

I sat in the front row, and the drums and music started. It was the praise and worship time, and everyone got up and danced and praised God and rejoiced. I looked and stared; I didn't quite understand everything going on, but I knew inside of me I wanted to experience the joy and liberty all those women were experiencing.

After the service was over, I ran to say hello to Mommy Aluma, and to let her know I made it. She was so delighted to see me; she encouraged me and asked me to come back often.

When I looked at the time, it was way past time for me to be home; it was almost 8 p.m. How do I explain my time away from home? I ran to the road and flagged down another bus that took me to the nearest stop on Vandikiyaa Street, and as I walked home, my dad had not yet come home from his trip, so I sneaked into the house and went straight into my room. I slept like a baby that night. I was experiencing the peace of God, but I didn't know it. I felt like I had no cares in this life.

I started to visit House of Mercy more frequently. One day as I was at the meeting, I sat in front at my usual spot and listened, and when we started to praise, I remembered getting up and joining in the praise, and the next thing I remembered I was being picked up from the floor. Mommy had laid hands on me and was praying for me when I slid to the floor. I am not sure how long I lay there, but when I got up, something was different. I cried like I never cried before. When the service was over, I was afraid of asking anyone for a ride home, so no one would recognize me or connect me to my family. As I got on the bus and got back home, this time I wasn't so lucky; my father had arrived home and was waiting angrily for me in the compound. It was way past 9 p.m. and everywhere it was dark. As I sneaked in through the side gate, the metal on the gates squeaked and made a loud noise. We learned later on to put palm oil on the hinges of metal doors so those horrible tell-on-you noises would go away, but not this time.

My dad called me and asked me to come upstairs to his room. As I walked up the stairs, he sat me down and asked me, "Where the 'Hell' are you coming from at this time of the night, leaving your baby at home?"

I didn't have an answer. If I said I went to a friend's house, he would want to know which one and find out before I was able to reach them; it was no use. If I said I was coming from church, he would say, "Today is not Sunday." I didn't know how to explain myself out of this one. So, I told him I went to House of Mercy, and he said, "What is that and where is that?"

I said, "It is a place where women go to pray, and it is not a church; I think it is a fellowship."

He said, "Today will be your last day going over there. You should be aware of what people are saying. I have been told you have been going out at night and coming back late; who knows what you're out there doing. Who do you want to convince that you're going to church? Everyone knows your husband just died, and you should not be seen outside, unless you go back to school next semester. You have not completed your mourning time, and you look very bad sneaking out like this. Do you know what your in-laws will say if they find out?"

I said, "Yes, sir! It's been almost 8 months and going to this meeting has been very helpful."

He said, "I don't know what you just said, but you will not go over there any more."

I went back to my room and I cried, and then I prayed and asked God to help me the best I could. I didn't go back to House of Mercy again for a few weeks. I read my Bible at home and talked to God the best way I could.

Time went by quickly. It was January again and time for a new semerster. I went back to school, but I was in class with a whole new set of people. My hair had grown about 4 inches. I was allowed to go to school with my hair uncovered, and I still wore drab clothes. I was still behind with school work, and at this point I wasn't interested in that environment any more; everywhere I went, the whispers continued; everyone stared at me. I was so uncomfortable.

One day I came back home from school and I sat in the compound. About dusk, my stepmother Ann had had a little brawl with my dad and decided to take it out on me. She walked past me and as she climbed up the stairs, she asked what I was looking at.

I said, "I wasn't looking at anything."

She said, "Oh well, I need to let you know that this house is not your house. Because your father allowed you to come back here after Paul died doesn't mean you should come sit down and have everyone serve you." Then she said, "Didn't you say you wanted to live in America? What are you still doing here in Makurdi?" and she mockingly laughed at me and went back into her room.

That night was the night I knew if nothing changed about my situation, I was going to take matters into my own hands. I had had enough; life was not fulfilling anymore, and I was not afraid of dying. I gave up on life long after my mom passed away, and my only means of escape from the dysfunction in my home was marriage; that too was gone, and now life was unrealistic. The pain was too much to handle. I was a twenty-four-year-old, living in a 60-year-old woman's body and mind, dealing with hard-core life issues when my mates were dating, traveling and seeking out careers for their futures. How did I end up in this mess?

I sat outside that night; the generator had been turned off and it was quiet and very dark. I could hear crickets and little night creatures, but it was an ugly night for me. From within me, I heard in my ears, *"It will be better if you die; you will have so much peace and don't have to worry about this life any more; no one will laugh at you any more, and no one will miss you either. Can't you see that you can't do anything right? You have made so many wrong decisions."* The more I thought about it, the better it felt. The voice was right: I made wrong decisions, and I cried, and as I cried harder, my dad heard me from his bedroom and came to the balcony and asked, "Who is that outside in the dark?"

I said, "It's me."

He said, "Why are you not sleeping?"

I responded, "I am tired of life and will take my life if I had the means."

My dad walked down the stairs, sat beside me in the compound, asked me never to repeat anything like that again and asked me to be strong for my daughter. He said, "If you die, who will take care of your daughter?"

I got up and walked to my room. My dad closed the door behind me, but I realized it took a while before I heard his footsteps walking away from my door.

It wasn't long before I went back to House of Mercy for another fellowship. My dad didn't have any problems with me going back again, but I tried to get back home before it was too late. As time went on, I met some amazing women at the fellowship that encouraged me. Mommy all the while encouraged me and asked me to join the usher team, so I did. We beautified God's house by hanging curtains, arranging seats or doing whatever was needed.

By March of the next year, Bishop Francis Wale Oke was coming to House of Mercy for a crusade, and Mommy had asked all of us to be expectant and ask God for our hearts' desires. I did ask God that I wanted to travel to America and start a new life.

The crusade was highly anticipated, and people flocked in from everywhere, both men and women. As ushers we had arranged everyone in their positions. Praise and worship were filled with God's presence, then Bishop Francis walked up to the microphone in the middle of the service. As he raised his hands, the music tempo slowed down, and he said, "I perceive there is a young woman in our midst that the devil wants to destroy; you recently lost your husband and....," as he kept on talking, he said, "I want you to step out now." I didn't leave my position even though I felt a nudge in my heart, and I didn't want to have any eye contact with Mommy Aluma, so I kept looking down at my feet. Two women walked up to the front toward the altar, and when he looked at them, he said, "No, not you." At that moment, Mommy and I looked at each other, and she beckoned me forward. As I walked toward the Preacher, he left the pulpit and walked towards me, and he raised his finger right into my face and as he did he exclaimed "YOU"? And he placed his hand on my forehead and started to pray in words I could not understand. Down on the floor I went. By the time I got up, I could not remember how I got there. I was helped back to my seat.

After the service was over, the ushers had to assist all the guests who travelled from their various locations. As we entered the car and I turned, I was sitting beside Bishop Francis Wale Oke and his assistant. He said, "Young lady, I see that you are desperate for God. What do you want from God?"

I said very childishly, "I want to go to America."

He said, "Do you know in particular the reason?"

I said, "I just want to start my life all over."

Then he spoke into my life, words that resonate till this day.

I was very excited, and I went by Mommy's house the next day to tell her all that I was told the night before. Then Mommy asked me if I really wanted to leave, and I told her yes. Then again, she prayed for me, and spoke into my life. She asked the Lord to wipe away my tears. She asked that God would beautify my life and send me a husband that would remain. She prayed that God would break every soul tie from my past marriage and make me whole again. She asked for God to establish me and keep me in safety, and like a mother, she blessed me and said it would be well with me. I took a little notepad and wrote all these words down and held it close to my heart. These words kept me going in the Journey of my life. I do have this notepad with me up until this day.

After a couple of months went by, the thought of traveling and relocating got stronger, and I decided to try out for visas. Tutu had turned two years old, and I had graduated from university the spring of that year. Paul had a couple of friends who had called, and some came by to visit me and the baby, but it wasn't long before the friends all disappeared. A few who stayed back tried to take advandtage of my fragile heart. One in particular was the best friend of Paul. I saw him as a go-to person, but his heart was wicked. He had started to visit too often, send gifts to the house and spend longer times when he visited, and talked about the stress he was having at home and on the job.

It wasn't looking good; I knew after a while that this was a trap. It wasn't long before I found out that I wasn't emotionally stable enough to handle any tricks. Everything that looked like sympathy and succor was welcomed, but it wasn't long before I started receiving threats and name-calling. When I went out to public gatherings, I noticed the wives would come and stand right in front of me when their husbands tried to say hello and to ask after my well being and how Tutu was faring. It was very humiliating to see how my position had changed.

In Nigeria, marriage is held in the highest honor, and women would remain in their marriages no matter what went on. Most Nigerian women will endure physical and emotional abuse just to maintain the marital status and will go to any extent to maintain the marriage. I was becoming a threat to our circle of friends; slowly but surely, I withdrew and remained on my own for the sake of peace and dignity. I knew I was no longer welcomed. Not long after those incidents, my father had gone out with a couple of his friends for a drink in a local thatched hut as was his usual manner, and as they sat down, the men around him didn't know that I was his daughter because it was dark, and my father did not talk a lot in public. He was a good listener and observed everyone around him. As they talked about me in the thatched house, one man said, "Have you seen that Obekpa's daughter? She is a black widow. No one should go to her; see what happened to that young man she married after one year?" And they kept on talking, but my dad spoke up when he could not handle that conversation any more; he said, "You all are talking about my daughter, and what you're saying is not fair." He stood up and left.

When he came home, he said, "I am not sure what your plans are, but this place is not good for you anymore." I was labeled, and the stigma for a twenty-four-year-old was too much.

Despite the odds against me, I graduated from University and had a few more months to work for my national youth service corp. Every University graduate in Nigeria had to go through the National Youth Service Corp. to work. While I waited for the youth service placement, I went to Mommy Aluma at the House of Mercy and cleaned or worked around the building.

Mommy started teaching me in the things of God, and how to fast and pray. I went back home in the afternoons. That was a time of spiritual growth as Mommy encouraged me to go to church on Sundays. I would go to Living Faith Winners Chapel on Sundays and would follow Mommy and others to any programme or crusade that was going on in the city—prayer meetings, deliverance meetings, etc., and I saw many miracles and healings take place. Then we would go for evangelism, and before long, I started telling others about Jesus. Once I stopped an okada for transportation, and when I reached my destination, I talked to him about Jesus. Before long, every okada bike I took, I told them to give their life to Christ. I would pray the prayer of salvation with them and pay them for the ride.

Before long, I started going to the hospitals to see the sick people, and that was how I encountered a young lady I'll call Abahi, whose life changed my life. It was at St. Theresa Hospital one Saturday morning as I walked from bed to bed. The missionary hospital had several beds in one long hall, not private rooms like America at that time; things are a lot different now. This girl was not more than sixteen years old, but I later found out she was older; she was pale and looked like the life in her was slipping away. I sat by her bedside, and I smelt a strong purulent odor closer to rotten flesh; that smell was the same smell my classmate had all around her in high school when she died. I could not help it, so I held my nose with my fingers, and I moved closer to the girl and asked her, "Why are you smelling like this?"

She looked at me with tears in her eyes and said to me, "I am dying from an abortion, and this is the punishment for my sins." I asked her if she knew Jesus. She said, "Yes, I am Catholic."

I talked to her about Jesus, and she gave her life to Christ. I told her about forgiveness and the love of Jesus, and I told her I would come back to visit her again. When I went back home, I could not take my mind off this young girl. I went back two days later, and she looked better and had some color returning to her skin. I was excited, and I kept going back to see her.

After seven days, she had been discharged from the hospital to go home. The smell had almost completely stopped, and I followed her to her house. She did not live very far from where we lived, so she became my friend, and I started visiting her quite often. I loved her like a sister and we formed a bond.

Back then, many young girls had died from committing abortions. They died to cover their shame; most of the victims never even notified who was responsible, and those who did were rejected by the men who were responsible. They covered up and were killed by quack doctors. (For the sake of my love and respect for your bravery, I will not call you by name in my book; my dear sister, if you're reading this book today, I just want to say I think about you and the wonderful life you're now living in Christ.)

Chapter 10: Transition

In the year 2001, I was tired of staying at home, and it looked like everything had come to a standstill. I had graduated from college and had stayed home for another year. I started to think about what the future held for me. As I sat down and pondered, I remembered the great land beyond the Atlantic, America, and I desired to go back to that land. I didn't know what I wanted to go back to America for, but I knew I had to go back. As the days went by, the feelings got stronger, and the desire to leave Nigeria and to start my life all over again loomed over me.

I remembered a friend of Paul who lived in Abuja; he was one of Paul's closest friends at the Federal Aviation Authority. I called him and asked if I could travel to see him. He was very gracious and invited Tutu and I over the next day. I boarded a taxi from Makurdi to Abuja. As we approached the city of Abuja, memories came flooding back that brought tears to my eyes—this used to be my home; this was the city where I was stripped of everything that caused me to glory in status. I was choking from the huge knot that had filled my throat, and as I started to cry, Tutu reached her hands to my face and wiped away the tears. She was only two years old and could not talk fluently; all she said was "Mommy crying?"

I said, "No, Mommy will be okay soon, and we are going to be okay."

We arrived at Mr. Akintola's house and were received by his wife. She offered us warm food and a place to stay over night. I told them I would love to stay but my sister lived in Abuja also and would gladly love to keep us. I would love to go by her place if he would be willing to drop Tutu and me off. After he ate, he did so, but he asked if there was anything he could do for us; he was willing to help me. I told him I wanted to relocate to America! He asked if I knew anyone living in America, because I would need accommodations, unless I just wanted to go for the holidays and think over my decisions and come back home.

I told him my older sister knew a couple of friends who lived there, and I was going to ask her to see if she could ask one of them to accommodate me. Mr. Akintola said that it was okay and that he was going to Lagos the following week and would fill out some forms for an American visa, and then when it was time for my interview, he would come with me to Lagos. I was so thankful after our conversation, that I thanked him for his kindness, and he dropped Tutu and me over at my sister's house.

I stayed with my elder sister for 2 days and then went back to Makurdi. A few months had gone by when I received a phone call from Mr. Akintola, that I would have a visa interview in November. He arranged to meet me in Lagos, so I told my father what I was planning to do. He probably did not believe me because I was the one child who stayed around the house most of the time.

I hated inconveniences, and this was a huge leap for me. He gave me transportation money and I traveled to Lagos to my uncle Joe's house. When we arrived in Lagos, I got a taxi from under the bridge to Isolo, where my uncle lived. When he got back later that evening, Tutu and I had been sitting outside for a good 3 hours; there were no phones available, so we just waited; it was about dusk when he arrived. He was shocked to see me because I didn't tell him I was coming. He took me into the house and told me it was dangerous to be on the streets of Lagos this late. We had warm showers and food to eat, then I told him that I was meeting with Mr. Akintola the next day at the American Embassy in Lagos.

So, the next morning I went to the embassy with Mr. Akintola. He paid the fees and asked me to sit and wait for my turn. When I was called up to the window, the lady asked me why I wanted to go to America. I told her I wanted to go on vacation. She looked down at me and stamped on my visa, "Denied." Funny how everyone was getting denied and no refunds were made for the fees paid.

I cried, and Mr. Akintola said he was sorry, he didn't know what else to do; he needed to get back on the plane to Abuja the following morning. As I stood by the gates of the Embassy, something inside of me said, "Go back and fill out another form and resubmit it." With tears in my eyes and a heavy heart, I pulled out another Visa application form, filled it out and placed it in the box. I hailed a taxi with the last money I had in my pocket to go back to my uncle's house. The next morning, my uncle took me to the bus station, and

Tutu and I took the longest nine-hour drive back to Makurdi. Words could not describe how I felt; I felt hopeless and disappointed. I felt like life was unfair and everything was working against me.

I got home that night and cried so hard I fell sick with a fever. My dad consoled me and asked me to brace myself, that it may not be the right time for me to go to America. He said I was making rash decisions because of the tragedy I was going through.

I continued normal life. I would wake up in the morning and visit the local hospitals and the orphanages behind our house; at mid-week I would go to House of Mercy to fellowship with the ladies; and gradually over a few weeks I started to regain strength. I hardly smiled, and I never did eat unless I remembered to eat. Mommy Aluma always encouraged me and told me to come to the House of Mercy and do whatever my hand found to do, so I would join the other ladies around to prepare the sactuary for the mid-week service, or I'd sit in the bookstore, and talk with the sales lady until it was time to go home. I bought some of my foundational books from that bookstore and I read those books over and over. I remember one of those books was *Good Morning, Holy Spirit* and *Welcome, Holy Spirit* by Pastor Benny Hinn.

It was so amazing to see what happened around the place; I was a new convert and didn't know much about healing, but I remember people were brought to the House of Mercy, laid in stretchers, and slept outside day and night, and after a few days they walked away healed, even HIV victims. I had seen a lady who camped out there on her deathbed outside for a few days until one night we had come for an all-night prayer vigil. We praised God and prayed from midnight until 6 a.m. All types of manifestations of the Spirit of God were evident. People were so hungry for the move of God and open to receive, no telling what happened in those services when people got their healing. The following week when I came by, the lady was no longer there; she was completely healed and quickened by the same power that raised Christ from the dead. I could go on and on to give an account of all that happened over at the House of Mercy. I am so thankful for the foundation I had because I would build on it when I started my journey in America. Thank you, Mommy Aluma, for answering the call.

Chapter 11: Predators

As the months went by, I gradually began to see how lonely life was becoming. All my siblings would come back for the holidays and go back to boarding school or various universities; I was the only one left at home most of the time. My older sister and cousins would stay in Abuja or Jos most of the time, but I had nowhere to go. A friend of Paul that we had known as a family friend started to visit the house very frequently. He was a man that we all loved and respected; he was at the time in his forties and I was twenty-four. He would come to the house after work and sit with Tutu and I and talk about Paul; he'd ask if there was anything he could do for us. He was not the only one who was visiting and checking, but he came by more frequently. He sent his drivers during the day to check on me and see how I was doing. Sometimes he would ask me if I wanted to take a walk, and I would go walking with him. His wife also had come by to visit me at home a couple of times; as young as I was and naïve, I didn't see anything wrong with it. However, I realized he started talking to me about his marriage when we went walking; it got very awkward. One day when he started talking about his wife in a bad light, she wanted to relocate to the UK, and spend all this money without making any income. In my heart I thought this lady was kind and friendly; I didn't see anything wrong with her; but then he'd make comments like, "You know, a man will leave his castle to follow a woman he loves."

I foolishly said, "Really?"

And he went on and on and on, and every day he comes by the house and we'd sit outside and talk; I found a companion. I wasn't quite sure what was going on in his marriage, but I knew this man was up to no good. I told him he needed to stay home with his wife, and I thanked him for his loyalty to his friend who was no longer with us.

It wasn't long before I began to receive threats from his wife, and I was accused of being a husband-snatcher. It seems like everyone that came around me wanted to take something from me; it wasn't long before I started to build walls around my heart. I started to grow tougher; I knew my dad could not protect me anymore. I knew I had to grow up fast to defend myself against predators to survive. I was no longer under the covering of a man. I was then mom and dad for my little girl, and I had to keep hurt away from her by all means possible.

Some of you reading this book may be wondering how I could be so naïve or what I was thinking in some of the chapters of this book. Well we grew up sheltered, strict, and had no experience in dealing with the world. My mom left home when I was thirteen. All that mattered in my home was education and discipline. The general belief was "we'll take care of it when we get there." When most of our mates were hanging out at the clubs, sneaking out to visit men and traveling out of the country without parental consent or going to government official VIP parties, we had no idea what that life was, so yes, I was twenty-five and naïve. Marriage does not equal maturity or worldly wisdom. When I look back after twenty-plus years, I am asking the same question: "What was I thinking?"

In December of the year 2000, I was at home, when I heard footsteps coming into our home. A young man, probably ten years older than I, walked into our house—I am not sure how he came in unnoticed—and said, "Good evening. My name is Captain Binda, and I have come to see you."

I said, "Yes; how can I help you?" In my heart I thought it was one of Paul's old friends who came to visit me.

He sat down and offered me a little purple suede bag with a satin rope around it. He said, "This is for you, please open it and don't reject it."

I opened the bag, and my eyes were so big I could not accept it without knowing why he was giving this gift. It was half full of uncut diamonds. I don't know where he got it from, but I knew in my heart I could not accept it. So, I told him I could not accept it, and I wanted to know why he was here and who sent him.

He said he came because he heard about me and wanted to ask my permission to marry me. I was so disgusted that I told him not to come back.

That night I had gone back to the fellowship and told Mommy Aluma what had happened. She advised me that I was young and had just lost a husband; there would be lots of temptations and so many people would come to take advantage of me. She prayed God's protection over me, and I went back home.

Two days later, I was sitting in the compound picking shells from a bowl of black-eyed peas when I heard my dad call me, in a voice I knew too well that something good had happened. I jumped across the stool and spilled the bowl of beans everywhere and ran to his office. He said, "This is the letter for you from the American Embassy." I was twenty-five years old, but my dad still had the privilege of opening my mail. He said, "You have an interview on January the 2nd, 2001." I was so thankful, I rejoiced. That was the best Christmas present. I didn't tell anyone about it, but I told Mommy Aluma, and she thanked God with me and asked God to order my steps and grant me favor. I was so happy.

Chapter 12: Visa

That Christmas, my cousins had come from Lagos to see their mom, my aunty in Otukpo. It was time for them to go back. I figured it would be a great opportunity to follow them back since I had an interview. In the morning of Janury 2nd, my brother-in-law took Tutu and me to the American Embassy and asked us to come back in a taxi. He wrote down the address of their house on a piece of paper and handed it to me. I carried Tutu on my right hip, and a shoulder bag on the left. She would cry and get irritated from all the long waits; looking back now, I can't imagine how she made it.

My number was called and as I approached the lady at the window, I said, "O God, please help me." She asked me a few questions and looked sternly at me and stamped my passport with a two-year multiple visa. It looked like I was dreaming. I got so excited I ran out with Tutu and hailed a taxi; as we entered the taxi, the taxi driver, an older man, looked at me and my baby and said, "Madam, you look like you are not a Lagosian; I can see that you have good news from the Embassy." He then said to me, "Hide that thing in your hand very well; God has helped you today. You can get killed for that in Lagos; people are looking for this thing you have in your hand, okay? Where are you going?"

I handed him the address, and paid him his money, and he took me to my cousin's house. I called my dad on the phone to tell him I was issued a visa; he was happy for me. I called Mr. Akintola to tell him the good news, and he was very excited.

Chapter 13: My Dad's Reaction to My Visa

When I finally arrived in Makurdi, my dad called me to his bedroom. I noticed his countenance had changed; he was not as excited as I thought he would be regarding the visa. I asked him if something was wrong or if I had done anything. He responded back to me in a low tone, and said, "Have you given good thought about this trip to America?"

I said, "Yes."

He said, "Do you really want to go to America?"

I said, "Yes."

He said, "You know, you're a single woman, and people will perceive you differently; they will think you are going to America to be a prostitute. You have never worked, you don't have a lot of physical skills, you graduated with a bachelor's degree, but that does not mean you can work with it. You don't have any accounting work experience outside of the classroom. Go and rethink your decision. I can find you a job next week in the Central Bank of Nigeria, one of the top banks here. I have friends I can call to make things happen, and after a year you can take your ICAN board exams: Institutes of Chartered Accountants in Nigeria. Then you can live your life and do what you want to do and make a good life for yourself and your daughter. I think that is the best plan. I will call Princess Olabunmi in the morning, and we can go out to see her in Abuja."

Words could not describe all the emotions that were running through me. I was numb; I could not believe what I was hearing. It felt like my balloon was deflated by a million needles (i.e., I was disappointed and discouraged). I said, "Okay, papa," and went into my room. I lay on my bed and cried till I fell asleep. When I woke up the next day, my eyes were bloodshot from crying and my lips were swollen. I told my dad I still wanted to go to America and I would be needing money for airfare, not only for myself but for Tutu.

Believe it or not, we took a trip to Abuja to see the famous princess who could wave her wand and change my life forever. She did oversee the bank. She was very rich and her house was built with marble interior, exquisite furniture, and hand-picked art work. She was a woman you would not forget when you met her. She had her hair in a traditional updo decorated with real coral beads; her wrist was decorated with coral beads and gold, and a gold ring was on every finger; with beautiful makeup, she carried herself well and walked delicately. She counted her steps; when she alighted from the owner's corner of her car, the drivers bowed before her to open the door. We walked into her living area, and she said, "Young lady, how are you and how can I help you?" She said, "We can talk after I have had dinner."

She asked me to go to the kitchen to bring her a glass of water, and as I walked into her kitchen she had at least 4 maids in there preparing her dinner. She lived alone; I did not see any husband or children anywhere. She rang the little bell beside her, and all four girls ran out and started kneeling before her. In my heart, I was thinking, *This is not going to work for me. I'm out of here as fast as I came in.* I walked back to the living room with her cup, and she asked me to kneel when giving her a glass of water. I told her, "I am sorry, ma'am, I can't kneel to give you water; I am not Yoruba. Let's try it next time." The cup was on the table by the end of my sentence.

She said, "Yes, so how can I help you and what brings you here?"

I told her, "I am Prince Gabriel Obekpa's daughter, and I think my father wanted you to find me a job in the bank, but I am not interested."

She said, "Okay, I'll let him know you're not interested."

I spent the night at her place but went back home the next day. I never saw that woman again until this day.

Chapter 14: Journey (Traveling out of Nigeria)

Two months had gone by after I received my visa; I wasn't working. I had my American visa in my hands but was doing nothing. By mid-February, I knew if I didn't make the move, that was the end of my traveling plans.

I had had enough. I sat outside one quiet night; the electricity was out, and the generators worked only until 10 p.m. I could not sleep, so I sat in the compound and I started to cry. I looked up into the sky as if I was looking for some type of an answer. The night was so quiet, I cried and sobbed until I began to wail.

My father came out and looked down from upstairs and asked what I was doing outside so late.

I told him I could not continue, and I threatened him that I was going to take my life if he did not let me leave. I told him my life was nothing, and I was tired of taking all the humiliation. No one from Paul's family after one year came by my father's house to ask after me or the baby. I walked around the street and people were staring at me; the younger ladies were making fun of me. Men were trying to take advantage of me, and I cried all the more. How long can I do this?"

He said, "Go back inside; it's too late now."

The following day about 6 p.m., my dad called me up to his room and brought out a huge baco supper sac, with red and white stripes filled with money. He placed it in front of me and said, "This is three-hundred-thousand naira, enough to cover your airfare and another four hundred pounds for your pocket money until you come back." My father blessed me, and with a heavy heart he realeased me to go. I thanked him and hauled that bag of money down the stairs. I folded one yard of Ankara fabric over the money and zipped up the bag. I took all the pictures I could carry—Paul's pictures, my wedding pictures, my mother's pictures, and a few family pictures, and I tied them securely in a plastic bag, and the next morning I was on my way to Abuja.

The Archbishop of the cathedral church in Gariki, Paul's church, had asked to see Ihotu and I because that was where we went to church in Abuja. Paul was a devout Catholic and was at mass every day and had a good rapport with the Archbishop.

When I went to see his holiness, as he was called at the time, he gave Tutu and me monitary gifts as condolence for Paul's death. We thanked him and kept on with our journey.

My sister in Abuja had contacted a friend's family in Atlanta, Georgia, and he talked with his wife, and they agreed to accommodate us. She gave me the address written on a paper, and I took it with me and boarded a taxi to Lagos. It was a very quiet exit. I called a few close people to let them know I was leaving, and I called Mommy

Aluma before I left Makurdi. I went to visit her that night; she blessed me, prayed for me, and asked me to keep in touch. I gave her a big hug and left.

I called Pastor Emma Opara; he came to visit me and brought some reading materials to me and asked me to keep them close to my heart and read them. Those books were key transformational turns in my Christian walk. He handed me the *Believers' Authority* by Kenneth E. Hagin. (I still have that book after sixteen years and still read it once every few years.) He prayed for me and asked me to pray and always keep in touch.

The journey to Lagos this time was not as smooth. We had traveled at night. The taxi had broken down twice in the middle of nowhere. I had my little two- almost three-year-old with me that was crying. We had been sitting in this cramped, overloaded taxi. We had stopped while it was still daylight to eat; I ate a little piece of black amala and ewedu soup. We had hardly enough water to wash our hands. A few hours later my stomach started to hurt, and I got sick, throwing up. The taxi driver was not pleased as he stopped the taxi for me to get comfortable. We arrived in Lagos, and as everyone pulled out their bags, the taxi driver lifted my bag and flung it to the ground. I bet he had no idea that that bag was filled with money.

As I tell this story, I look back to see how God protected me. I pulled this bag of money off the wet muddy floor, and with my little bag on the other side and Tutu on my hip, I hailed a cab, and went to my uncle's house in Isolo. When I arrived, his wife Henrietta offered us a room to stay in, a shower, and asked us to rest till morning. By morning, I told my uncle, "I was on my way to the US, and papa finally gave me money for my ticket."

He said, "I am so happy for you, Onyi. I'll ask my wife to call the travel agency to see what available tickets they have." He asked to see the check I had. I told him it was in the room and I could go get it. When I came out of the room dragging a Baco supper sack with me, my uncle got up from the chair and could not believe what he was seeing. He then asked, "Is this how you came from Makurdi?"

I said, "Yes. I actually went to Abuja before coming to Lagos."

He was in so much shock, he called his wife in horror to come out and see what was happening. I was so naïve; I thought, *"Why are they overreacting?"* It was later on I realized how much of a mistake and how much of a risk I had put myself and my baby through, in coming to Lagos in a public transport with a bag filled with cash. It is not done!

The following day my uncle's wife made arrangements and bought flight tickets for me and Tutu, and added the money left over to my pocket money. The day my tickets were handed to me, I started developing cold feet. Fear came in, and for the first time I started having second thoughts about traveling. I started thinking, *"What if I go to the airport and I get turned back or am deported? How about if they ask me where I'm going with this child and where her father is?"*

173

The thoughts started to fill my heart. I spent a whole week in Lagos. One night while I slept, I had a dream my Visa was taken from me. I woke up sweating. I had worked myself up so much I was having dreams; I could no longer take it. I talked to my uncle that I was afraid and had been having all these thoughts.

He asked me to be bold and just know that everything would be alright. On March 2nd, 2001, my uncle and his family were going to Shiloh for a mid-week service, and on their way, they dropped Tutu and me at the international airport in Lagos. My uncle asked me to call him when I arrived in the U.S. He blessed me and waved good-bye to me.

It was about 5:30 p.m., and we didn't have to board until 9 p.m., so for the remaining 3 hours, Tutu and I sat in a spot and looked at people as they came and went. We had little to eat. At 9 p.m., when the call came, I had no bag to check in except for the little carryon I had and a little diaper bag for Tutu. I was so thin—I weighed about 125 pounds at 5 ft. 9 inches tall. I had a little red t-shirt on with Mickey Mouse drawn on it, and dark blue dungaries. I stuffed my ticket and my passport in the front pocket of my overalls because it was easy to reach. I had my money tied in a little strap bag across my waist, to be not as noticeable.

As we boarded the plane and took our seats, Tutu was too scared to sit by herself, so I had to carry her on my legs, and as the plane taxied in line on the runway getting ready to lift off, I looked through the

174

window and two big warm tears rolled down my cheeks. I was separated from my family, I was separated from the life I once knew, I was going into the unknown, I was so scared, I was by myself, and, now I can say God was with me all along; I just didn't know it. I felt a relief, I didn't know what was ahead of me, but one thing I was sure of. I needed a change, and at that moment that was all I was thankful for.

A deep sleep came over me. The next time I woke up we had arrived in Amsterdam. Tutu and I had missed all the meals in the plane and could not remember the last time we ate. We grabbed our stuff and headed for the exit. As our passports and paperwork were scrutinized by security, we saw other people being turned back, or they were not allowed to get off the plane. I did see a young man that had entered the plane with me from Nigeria; he was escorted away by security. I didn't know what was going to happen to me. As I handed my passport to the security lady, she spoke a language I didn't know or understand; it was in Dutch. She gave me back my passport, smiled at Tutu, and asked me to move on. I walked quickly across the checkpoint. It is amazing how fear was working on me—I had legal papers, I had my American visa stamped by the embassy—but yet I was so afraid; my mindset was now geared towards the thought that anything good I had was going to be taken from me. I didn't know how or when, but I had the mindset that nothing good was going to last. Tragedy had changed my perception. As we walked into the huge airport, the cold in Amsterdam was no joke; we had no winter coat and it was freezing. I walked to a shop and asked for Coca-cola. I took two bottles and handed the man the money in my hands, and he said, "We don't accept that or pounds." He showed me a place where I could change foreign currency, but by the time I could do all that, it was almost time for me to board another plane to America. By this time, Tutu was too weak to cry, and I was too tired to care, so we walked the long way to the next terminal, waiting to board.

The announcement came from the overhead, and it was time to board the plane to America. Whatever was turning in my stomach was not as gentle as butterflies; I was ready for the last huddle. I picked up Tutu, we got cleared and got into the plane. As we took our seats, the plane was packed full; it was a Boeing 747 "jumbo jet." Everyone looked excited and friendly. The airliner was packed with Americans and a few foreigners. It wasn't long before the air hostesses made sure everyone was comfortably seated. Then the captain welcomed everyone on board, and you could tell the pride in his voice for his country; he was an American. The safety routines were done, and off we went.

Tutu never got used to the planes taking off; she always screamed and tried to get out of her seat, which drew attention to us. This time the air hostess came to calm her down and gave her a lollipop, and the fear disappeared. I didn't know a lollipop could cast out fear; I needed a dozen. It wasn't long before we had a light snack, but I realized I had no appetite. Tutu was able to eat, and she slept all through the journey. It was a whopping nine hours and 30 minutes of flight. I

176

looked through the window most of the time; I looked in the sky and looked down as we flew across the Atlantic Ocean. I could not read nor sleep; I did not watch any videos; all I thought about was my life and what was in store for me. The future was unknown.

Chapter 15: Early Days in Atlanta

America is a land seen by so many people as the land flowing with milk and honey, that most people have dreamed about leaving their home country for a better life. People migrate from all over the world for the American dream, but with no real picture of what to expect. Leaving Nigeria and moving to America for me in my present circumstances was an answer to all my problems. It was going to be a new and fresh start. I didn't count the cost of the adjustments I had to make, the culture shock and the compromises that go along with migration. The journey for so many leads to disappointment, and psychological and mental breakdown. As the years go by, so many people are too ashamed to go back home, so they stay, living a life of poverty and hiding from the Authority. So many undocumented immigrants have been lost in the society and have not been able to rise; it takes money to go through the legal and immigration system and a whopping four to seven thousand dollars if not more to file the right paperwork with an immigration attorney. This is not counting the years it takes to have all the paperwork approved. It is illegal to work and make a living during this period. As immigrants continue to flock into the promise land, they are met with these challenges and become afraid to ask for help. Most people are ashamed to go back home, so they continue to live with the hope that maybe one day it will get better.

Immigrants are faced with acculturation issues, they have come to a land with different cultural practices, they stand out like a sore thumb, they have a different accent, and the pressures of discrimination are right in their faces daily. Most of the immigrants after a while become lonely and are homesick; it is difficult to get around' transportation is difficult, and so they maneuver their way through the system. The immigrant at this point will have to make a cultural shift to adapt to the dominant culture. Most people have to find odd jobs, in the farms, cleaning and washing dishes in the hotels and restaurants, factory jobs and whatever they can find their hands to do, but as the years go by, the American dream begins to dwindle and immigrants get desperate, the pressure mounts and as some make bad choices for survival, others keep hope alive and wish that it will get better someday.

It was a huge change for me, the culture shock was no joke, I had to make a shift in my paradigm. I had to set aside all that I once knew about what living was, to survival mode. I had left the comfort of my home and my familiar environment to a new land. I just wanted to get away from the pain and start allover.

We arrived at Hartsfield-Jackson International Airport in Atlanta, Georgia. The plane was emptied, and everyone was asked to go through Immigration. The Atlanta airport had a different vibe to it; it was lively, the people were very friendly, and they were glad to see the people come through. They had a different line for American citizens and another line for immigrants.

As I continued walking along the hallway, I saw a bathroom and I took Tutu with me inside the bathroom. I sat there for about 10 minutes. I was too scared to go through Immigration; the dream I had before I left Lagos came back, and fear gripped me. *"Now this is my final destination, but I think they will send me back."* As I mustered the last strength in me, I walked out of the bathroom, and the lines had almost been cleared out when I quickly walked up to the immigration counter. The lady looked at me with a very disturbing look and said, "Young lady, where are you coming from and where in Atlanta are you going?"

I was shaking so much my passport fell from my hands to the floor; as I picked it up to give to her, I dropped Tutu on the floor, and as I turned to respond to the immigration officer and handed her my passport and the address of the people I was going to be staying with, Tutu ran through the tapes and started running off. She ran through the lines that said, "Welcome to Atlanta." As I turned to Tutu and started calling her name, the immigration lady was a little scared for me losing my child, so she quickly stamped my passport and asked me to hurry up and go pick up my child. I said, "Thank you."

Tutu had run across the line; I was a long way behind, so I increased my strides and caught up with her. I swooped Tutu from the floor. I didn't look back until I was downstairs by the train station. After a sigh of relief, I asked some people around me for information, and some were kind enough to stop and talk to me. I gave them the phone number in my hands; they showed me the phone, and I called the number. A male voice answered the phone, and I told him who I was and that I had arrived America. He said he would be out there to get me in 30 minutes, and to wait for him. He gave me directions to where I should wait, and I did, and he came to get us. He stretched out his hands to pick up my bag and said in the thickest Igbo accent I have ever heard—for a second I thought I was in Onitsha— "Hello, my name is Uche Dala. Welcome to (Amerika) America!"

I nodded my head and said thank you. We arrived at his home after a thirty-munite drive. I looked through the window all through the drive and was already missing home. We stopped at a gas station to pick up a prepaid calling card. I could not wait to call home to let them know I had arrived safely. We were welcomed at the door by 3 little screaming kids and a stout woman with a high-pitched voice; she welcomed me and helped me into a guest room. I told her I needed to make a phone call to my family, and very quickly I called my dad and my sisters to let them know that I had arrived safely. They were all very excited; my dad advised me to make sure I called frequently, and I said, "Yes papa, I will." When I hung up the phone, it didn't occur to me that it would take another 12 years before I'd see my dad again. I took a shower and changed into comfortable clothes, but I didn't come down again until the next day.

I came down the stairs and as I looked around it just dawned on me that I was finally in America. The streets across had beautiful houses with people walking their dogs outside. People didn't really speak to each other. Then I heard a voice behind me, "How was your night?" It was Tamara, Uche's wife.

I said, "I slept well, thank you."

She said, "Come and let me show you around the house." She took me to the kitchen and showed me the pantry and the washing machine and so on.

Uche came down the stairs with a cigarette in his hands and said, "Nn'e, how are you?" (Meaning "young girl" in Igbo.)

I said, "I am doing fine, sir, thank you."

He said, "This is America; stop answering me 'sir'; just call me 'Uche.'" As he walked out the door, I noticed he didn't even acknowledge his wife nor did his wife acknowledge him. She went right back to what she was doing and started telling me about America. It looked like she had not had much companionship and had to tell all her story in 20 seconds. I smiled and listened, and not long afterwards I had to leave to go back to my room; I had nothing much to talk about. I allowed Tutu to play with the little children, and I stayed in my room. I didn't eat much and didn't know anyone. I had no email address, and the computer was not even anything I knew how to use before I came to America. I came down to get some water from the kitchen, and then I overheard Uche on the phone talking to a friend, saying, "You will not believe it, they just brought me a young wife from Nigeria."

I thought I was hearing things, and as he kept on in the conversation, I went back upstairs, and I said to myself, *"What is going on? Why would he refer to me as a wife from Nigeria?"*

By evening we all were watching TV and Destiny's Child came up on the TV singing, "I'm a survivor, am not gonna give up, am not gone...," and all the kids and Uche joined in like it was the national anthem, and I just kept looking after the music was over. He said, "Don't you know this song? This is Destiny's Child, and that's Beyonce," and he went on and on.

Then I said, "I don't know it," even though I did; I was trying to avoid any conversation.

He said, "You look like you are one of those church people; anyway, welcome to America."

I didn't say a word back to him. It was on Friday and I knew it would be Sunday in two days. I asked if they went to church and that I would like to go to church. He said he didn't go to church and his wife didn't drive, so she didn't go to church either. He said, "Do you know of any church around here you want to go to?"

I ran upstairs and pulled out the little notepad I had; all my important information was in there. Mommy Aluma had told me if I stayed in Atlanta to go to World Changers, so I handed him the name, and he said, "Oh, you want to go to Creflo Dollar's church?" Then he laughed and said, "I'll take you on Sunday, but I won't be able to do it every Sunday."

I was so excited! By Sunday morning, I was ready, and we took a 30-minute drive to World Changers. He dropped me off and said he'd come back to pick me up. The service was different from what I was used to back home; that was my first time seeing pastor Creflo Dollar outside of the TV screen. I gave him undivided attention. I sat about 4 rows from the front. The choir and everything was amazing. I lifted my hands for first-time visitors, and I was given some information that would be my saving grace later. Uche drove back to pick me up, and while we were driving home, he looked at me and said, "You know, you're a fine girl!"

I said, "Thank you, Uncle."

He said with a stern and angry tone, "Don't call me Uncle; call me Uche."

I said, "Okay," and tried to swallow the big nut in my throat. I started asking questions in my heart: *"What have I gotten myself into?"* It was an awkward drive back home.

When we arrived, I went back upstairs, and Tamara came up to my room. She asked, "Are you okay? And how was church?"

I said, "I am fine, thank you." I didnt want to start anything, and in my mind, I said, *"Nothing happened,"* and I told myself not to make a mountain out of a mole hill, for now I had nowhere to go. Then fear

184

started to come back. Tamara knew something was wrong; she was probably thinking, *"This young lady is weird."* I was awfully quiet and very reserved, so the next day I told her I was sorry for not being friendlier. I told her, "I lost my husband about a year ago, and life has since never been the same. I am only here in America to rest and think of what I am going to do next."

She said, "No problem; everything is going to be okay." It wasn't too long, about one week later, that Tamera had told all her Atlanta girlfriends she had a young girl from Nigeria to help her around the house. She started a business with her friend Lisa, an American girl from St. Louis. Lisa was married to Uche's friend Emmeka, another Igbo man, and they both drove Limosine taxis for a living. Lisa came by to see me and was happy that she and Tamera were finally starting to run their business, since it looked like they'd have a babysitter and a housekeeper now. They turned the little corner spot into a mini-office and bought furniture, typewriters and printers, and a telephone. Everything was going well, as planned. Tamera even borrowed the money I had brought with me from home to invest in her little business and promised to pay me later. Tamera was begging her husband to allow her to go out to the grocery store since she never did that before I came; she had an infant baby about nine months old when I came. Things were beginning to look brighter.

They had found house help—well maybe not exactly—I cooked and cleaned, and baby sat, not like that was a problem, but I was getting the wrong message. Uche just referred to me as a young wife, and now his wife was telling her girl friends they just sent her help from back home. Not too long afterwards, women started coming for me to braid their hair; they would drop me off at a friend's house to braid and pick me up after 10 hours or more. I didn't know how to braid hair from Nigeria, but I was a fast learner and did whatever I was told to do for the first few weeks. I remember I went to one lady's house to do her hair; she was a Nigerian lady named Cathy, a high roller in Atlanta. Her husband was an attorney, and when I finished her hair, she wrote me a check for $150 that I never cashed. Anyway, the reason I mentioned her was, while I was doing her hair in the basement of her mansion, she called her friend, Tamara (Uche's wife), and spoke in the Hausa language, a dialect used in the northern part of Nigeria. I could not speak fluent Hausa, but I was born in Jos, and went to the university for a little bit in Jos. My mother and my father spoke fluent Hausa. I lived in Abuja, and Hausa was the universal language after English. Transactions in the marketplace were in Hausa, so yes, I understood Hausa and could speak enough Hausa to get by. She said to Tamara, "Are you in your right mind? Why would you allow a beautiful young girl to come live in your house?" And as they continued and finished their conversation, I didn't say a word since I didn't want to give myself away. I couldn't hold back the tears as I sobbed; she didn't know I was sobbing because I was over her head braiding, and the tears kept falling on my shirt. I finished her hair and Cathy called Uche to pick me up. This was day eleven of my living in America.

As I entered the car with Uche, he said, "You are extremely quiet; are you okay?"

I said, "Yes, I am fine. As we started driving, it was about a 15-minute drive back home, but I realized twenty minutes had gone by. Then I said, "The drive is a little longer than normal," but what I didn't realize was that Uche had leaned closer to where I was sitting on the passenger's side and had placed his right hand on my thigh. I screamed and told him, "If you try anything, I will open this car on the highway and jump out!"

I started crying, and he said he was sorry and drove another five minutes. He stopped the car a few blocks before we reached home and asked me to stop crying and to wipe my face because Tamara would ask me what was going on, and I would be a fool to tell her what had just happened, because she would not believe me, and besides this is America, this is not a place for goody two shoes; he said, "If you agree to be my girl friend, I will rent an apartment for you and Ihotu, well furnished and no one will have to know. I can take you there next week and tell my wife I don't want you and the baby staying with us anymore."

I told him what he was doing was not right. I told him I just lost my husband and the emotions were still raw. I asked Uche to look how short the hair on my head was; it was a symbol of a woman who just lost her husband. I told him I just completed mourning and my heart was grieved; I didn't want to get into all this. I told him I didn't want to destroy his home. I told him his wife had been kind to me and trusted me, and I just needed a place to stay for a little while, and then I would be out of their home as soon as I could find an alternative arrangement.

Without any sympathy in his eyes, he said, "I'll give you a few days to think about what I just told you." Then he said, "My wife is fat and ugly; all she knows how to do is have babies."

I told him it was not my business, but it was his place to tell her exactly how he felt. He lit up a cigarette and drove all the way home with no word spoken. Now it'd been well over 45 minutes when I walked into the house. I picked up Tutu and walked up the stairs to my room and cried. I noticed Tamara didn't come to my room but went straight to Uche, and before I knew it an argument started. I didn't open my door; I slept till the following day. I didn't know where to turn. I couldn't use the phone because someone would hear my conversation. I managed to find a number for a friend, Nyechi, who lived in Canada. I called her, and I spoke my native dialect. She had lived in Canada and she could help me understand what was going on. I spoke my dialect to her and told her that my aunt lived in Ontario. She was excited because she happened to know my aunt and gave me my aunt's phone number. Nyechi told me I was in a bad situation, and if anything happened to me to call 911. I told her I didn't have anywhere to go, and I didn't want to go back home to Nigeria. She said not to worry that the police would take care of me. I also gave her the phone number of the house I was staying in.

One day Uche had gone out with his family, leaving Tutu and me in the house. I picked up the phone and called the phone number that was printed on the back of the World Changers' flyer. I told them I needed to talk to someone, anyone about my situation. They told me I could come by the next day because their offices were open, and they could send a church van to pick me up on Sundays for services. I was so thankful, and the next day I went out to the church office to talk to one of their church counselors. I told the lady my situation and I needed to know what to do to get out. She said I could leave and come to one of the houses for women in danger, and she prayed with me. I went back home but could not think of how to leave Uche's house with Ihotu to go to a shelter, coming from Nigeria. I did not understand the ways of the people, I had just been in America for 2 weeks; things started getting complicated.

The tension in the house was growing, but Uche had a better plan. I had not given him an answer and he decided to take matters into his own hands. I was sitting in the living room or in the kitchen, and Uche came and said to me, "Have you thought of what I told you?" He had the boldness to put his hands over my shoulders.

That same night while we all sat in the living room, he told his wife he had a friend coming in from Birmingham, Alabama, who could get a Social Security Number for this Nne (meaning "young lady" in Igbo), because he wanted me to be independent. Tamara said, "O that will be great; she needs to be independent."

189

I turned and looked at Uche and said, "I have only been in America for 2 weeks; I have a 2-year visa and am not sure if I am going to stay. Why do I need a Social Security Number?"

Then he said, "We can't continue to keep you here indefinitely. If you decide to stay, you will need a Social Security Number to work, or drive," and he kept on talking.

Finally, his wife said, "Okay, Uche, she doesn't understand how it works; you don't have to yell to talk, so when are you supposed to take her?"

He said, "Tomorrow morning."

At the time, I didn't know that a Social Security Number was issued from the Government. I didn't know how the system worked, and I was going along with the plan. Uche was also a limosine taxi driver and didn't have to clock in or clock out. I cannot remember his company; he had said he worked for the Gallaria, an Atlanta-based limousine company, something of that nature.

He had another friend, Amos, who came by the house to visit that evening; he was the better of the trio. I noticed he called Uche outside and was talking to him. Uche was laughing and puffing his cigarettes, but I noticed Amos was serious in his conversation.

I never knew what they had talked about, but by morning, Uche woke up bright and early to take me to this so-called friend coming from Birmingham. We drove to a Social Security office, and he said,

"Before I take you to my friend's office, let me show you how difficult it is to obtain a Social Security Number in America." At this point I was confused.

As he pulled up by the Social Security office, I got down from the car, walked into the building, and filled out a form. I was called to a window and asked by one of the officers, "Mem, why do you need a Social Security Number?"

I told her, "I was in America on vacation and had been here for 2 weeks." I showed her my passport that I was here legally and had a multiple-entry visa for 2 years.

She said, "Sorry, mem, I cannot issue you a Social Security "("SS") Number because of the following reasons…"

I said, "Thank you," and walked out the door. Then I told Uche, sitting in his car, what I was told.

He said, "Get in the car; let's go." As we continued to go, he said, "You will need an SS Number; you may not need it now, but you will need it later."

Cathy called to check on how we were doing for the day. And he answered the phone and said, "Everything is fine, and we will be home in a few."

He then pulled up in this neighborhood. At the time it looked nice and expensive—people were jogging and walking their dogs; huge houses were all made of brick. As he pulled by, I said, "Didn't you just tell Aunty we would be home in a few? We have already been to the Social Security office, and they said I can't have one. Why do we have to go to get one from your friend? Is that not supposed to be illegal? Please, I don't want trouble in this country."

He looked at me and hissed and then said, "You are foolish." We walked into the house and he said, "My friend is waiting; he needs to get your signature so he can process your SS number."

I said, "But we just left the official office and they said 'No.' Didn't you hear what I told you in the car?"

He said, "That was the official way, but there are other ways of getting it."

Then I told him, "I don't have a good feeling about this."

He said, "It will be quick, and if you don't want to sign it, you don't have to. He just wants you to try, because this is the way that everyone who comes to America does the same thing, and you will understand in a while."

As we walked into the house, a male voice said, "Hello, my name is ????." (I can't even remember what he said his name was.) He greeted Uche, and they laughed and shook hands. He said, "I'll be back. Let me run upstairs and I'll get my briefcase. I'll be right back." He was gone 5 minutes, then 10 minutes; the silence in the house got awkward. This man never returned.

Then Uche got up from where he sat and sat beside me. The light bulb just came on, and I realized that I was trapped; this was a set up. It had nothing to do with a Social Security Number! Uche pounced on me, and as I struggled with him, I started screaming at the top of my lungs, "Please no, no, no; please no; I can't; please no. In the name of God, Uche, please No." As I screamed, I was like a wild tiger; I was uncontrollable. How I got out of his grip I could not tell; I am sure he let me go. Uche was a big guy; he was of a good height and weight; I was no match for him. But I was out the front door, running in the neighborhood. A few people turned to look at me, but no one cared to stop me and ask if I was okay. I guess it is the American mindset—people did mind their business unless it would be a heroic action caught on camera and published in the news. Or maybe I was seen as another angry dramatic black woman on the street. I was shocked at everyone. As I stopped running to catch my breath, a black limousine pulled right beside me, and Uche said, "Get in the car, stupid girl."

I got in the car and I said, "I don't care what will happen to me today, but when I walk into the house I will tell Cathy what you have been doing. I can't take this anymore."

He said, "You can try, you fool." On the way home, Cathy kept calling, but Uche would not answer her call. When we finally got home, I walked up to the room, and came back down to the kitchen. I told Cathy all that had been happening, and I wanted to let her know because I could not continue like this.

She said, "I knew it! Idiot, I should have listened to my friends; they said I should not let you stay here. It is not Uche's fault, it is your fault, because your husband died; you want to come and take mine, evil girl," and as she rained on me, her 5-year-old son and 6-year-old daughter kept running around me screaming, "Mommy said you're the devil, devil aunty, devil aunty." And as they continued, Tutu kept looking at me with her wide eyes and didn't know what was going on.

I walked out the front door alone and began to walk; I can not say exactly for how long I walked, but I walked until I got lost. The next time I saw myself, I was in front of a Wal-mart store. My legs were swollen and hurting, and as I turned to go back home I could not find my way back. I stopped to ask a lot of people how to get back home, but everyone gave me a different direction. I remember leaving home about 3 p.m., and it was dark and almost 7 p.m. when I asked the last person for time and direction.

I walked, and as I got close to a familiar area, I remembered a house that I had visited with Uche and his family. I knocked on the door, and the lady of the house opend the door for me. She asked me why I was outside by myself, and I told her what had happened. I had taken a walk and was going back now. She said she was sorry to hear what had happened to me, and she asked me to be calm. I knew I could not stay there for too long since it was getting dark. She didn't offer to take me back, so I continued walking.

By the time I arrived home, almost 8 p.m., I saw over 10 cars parked in front of Uche's house. The men were outside smoking and the women were gathered inside. When I walked pass Uche and his friends, he said to Lisa's husband, "That's the foolish girl going in. Cathy will finish her in Atlanta; she has no clue." As I walked in, Cathy pulled me by my blouse and asked me to sit in the chair in the middle of a bunch of women. As I sat down, the first person I saw was the lady whose house I'd just left about 45 minutes before. She got to the house before me. And there was the lady that gave me a bad check from braiding her hair. It was like I was in a local courtroom awaiting trial and sentencing. Cathy stood up and said in her high-pitched voice, "Look at the stupid girl I brought from Nigeria. She has come to snatch my husband," and all the women clapped, screamed, and pushed, insulted, and called me all kinds of names. My daughter was sitting on the stairs watching all this happening, but her little 2-year-old mind could not make sense of the situation.

When Cathy walked up to me the second time, she showed me a new diamond ring Uche had picked up earlier that day. She said, "Look at my hands; he bought me this ring today. He loves me, and there is nothing anyone can do to snatch him away." I was in too much shock to say a word. I stood up from there and went to my room upstairs. Cathy came to me and said, "You have to leave now, right now, I mean like now."

I packed my stuff in my mini-bag and begged her to please stop yelling at me for the sake of my child. I asked if I could use the

195

telephone to make a phone call, but she said no. I told her I didn't have any money and she had not given me back the money she took from me. She ran upstairs and threw a $20 bill at me. I walked back out so I could get to the nearest gas station to make a phone call and buy a calling card. As I walked, every dignity was stripped off me; I experienced what shame truly was; I was beyond humiliation.

I was now bitter, and at that moment if I had had the means, I would have killed Uche and damned the consequences, and it would have been worth it. I hated men for how much power and control they had. My life changed in one instance. Lisa's husband stood there looking at me, without saying a word. I heard my father's voice in my head, "I told you not to go out there as a single woman, but you wouldn't listen." Then I was angry at Paul for putting me in this situation. I missed my mother. Everything that could go wrong had gone wrong. I made it to the gas station; I called my Aunty in Canada and told her what was happening. She asked me to call her back in 10 minutes. She knew a couple in Greensboro that could keep me until she could get me over to Canada. I called Amos; I remember he had secretly given me his number, the day he had talked with Uche outside, so that if I needed help to call him. I knew I was in a bad situation but didn't say anything about it. Maybe that was the conversation he was having with Uche that night and gave me the number before he left. Amos answered the phone; it was almost 10 p.m. at night; he said he would be there right away. I called my aunty back, and she gave me some phone numbers and asked me to leave and go to Greensboro, North

196

Carolina. She asked me to call the couple to pick me up from the bus station in the morning.

By the time I walked back from the gas station, Amos was already waiting for me. Tutu was sitting on our luggage by the door. I picked her up, and we never looked back. While driving with Amos, I broke down and started crying hysterically. He said he was sorry and had warned Uche not to do what he did. I didn't respond. As I came up to the bus, Amos took my luggage and bought a greyhound ticket for me and Tutu for $60 and left us there.

(Uche, you know your name has been changed to honor your children. I pray that you do not reap what you sowed. I do forgive you!) (Cathy, I hope you read this Book and see exactly what your husband, the father of your children, thinks about you! I pray you find your self-worth!)

The Greyhound bus left Atlanta that night and traveled the whole night with several stops. For the first time in my life, I was so nervous I could not hold my bowels. And I got very sick in the bus. I could not think or process anything I was so overwhelmed with grief, pain and sorrow. As the bus arrived Greensboro after twelve hours, it was cold, although it was almost April; coming from Nigeria it was very cold. I had no winter coat, neither did Tutu. I asked the people at the bus station for quarters to make phone calls. I had only one call to make, so I called the number my aunty gave me. The lady that answered said her husband didn't tell her I was coming, but she would not leave me in the cold, so she would come out to the bus station to get me. When we got to her home, I took a hot shower and gave Tutu a warm bath. Her name was Helen; she had 3 children at the time, 9, 7 and 4 years old. Her kids were adorable and immediately took a liking to Tutu. They lived in a modest rental property with 2 rooms and one bath. Tutu and I shared one room with her 3 children. The whole family was very gracious to us, but after my first experience, I would be indoors in the room every time the man of the house came home. He worked all the time, so he was never around anyway. I never did tell Helen my experience in Atlanta; I only told her I was on my way to Canada.

After a week had passed, the man of the house offered to take Tutu and I to the Canadian embassy in Washington. We drove 4 hours from Greensboro. When we arrived at the Canadian embassy, they denied me the visa. I called my aunty and told her I could not come.

At this point I started considering calling my dad to say, "You were right, and I was wrong; I want to come back home." Something in me would not let me do it. It looked like I was going to be with this family for a while.

Before leaving Nigeria, I didn't know that life in America was going to be like this. America for me was Sesame Street, Hollywood movies, big cities like Chicago and San Fransisco, Florida, New York, and Disney-world. Greensboro was not even in the picture!

Greensboro was rural; everything was small. The people talked with a Southern drawl; it was very different.

My life in America was just about to unfold and the reality of my choices was beginning to unfold. I never was the one who sat down to think of what I do. I was very spontaneous. I started thinking in my head, *"Do I remain in Greensboro? Do I go back home to Nigeria?"* But the constant question I could never answer was, "Go back to what? I had to go back to my father's house, marry an older man with other wives who would marry me because he felt he was doing me a favor, or just be nothing and live in the city. I really had no big dreams at this point; I was downcast.

I continued to live with this family and did all that I was asked to do. I didn't say much, and it was getting difficult for me to socialize. I had gone through so much pain and disappointment that I didn't trust anyone. One day in the fall, the couple had talked to me about meeting someone who lived in California, a cardiologist who was almost 20 years older than I was; they planned to buy me a plane ticket to fly out to visit this man. I thanked them but said I wasn't interested. They were doing the best they could to make me comfortable, and after a while it was very obvious it wasn't working. I cried a lot and stayed in the room all the time. Once in a while I'd come out to sit on the front porch when the man of the house was not home and would go back into the room when he came back. Their children were very respectful. I would braid their hair when I did Tutu's, and Helen would take me to the mall with all the kids or to the park.

About two months had gone by. When it was time for the couple's anniversary, they had gone out to dinner and I kept the kids. We played, and we were actually having a good day. When the couple arrived home, they called me and said they had something they needed to talk to me about. My stomach sank, but at this point it could not be anything worse. While I was living with this family, my aunty would call to check and see how I was doing and was very thankful to them; she had also sent a box of clothing to Ihotu, and her first winter coat was a cheetah leather and faux fur coat. She used that coat for the next 3 years; when she grew out of it, I took out the buttons and sewed on velcrow to extend the closure and I loosened the hem until the coat could not stretch any longer.

Because of all that I had gone through, I had lost a lot of contacts; I stopped calling home as much, I didn't call Mommy Aluma, and I just could not bring myself to tell anyone my situation. I could not afford to buy clothing or personal care items. I had to depend on the family I lived with to give me anything; it was very humiliating. Even though I was grateful, I didn't know how long I could cope with it, but I kept holding on.

As I sat on the couch to the right of Helen, her husband looked at me and said he wanted to thank me for all the help I had provided since I started living with them. He said they had bought a new home in Jamestown, and my eyes beamed with joy. In my heart, I started thinking, *Wow, we will go to better living conditions and I'll get a room to myself and maybe...* And as these thoughts came running through my mind, he then said, "Unfortunately we'll not be able to move with you and Tutu. The bills are getting high and you will have to find a place to stay." Then he said, "An alternative could be that you can get a roommate. And we know this guy named Emmanuel who works in a factory at Proctor and Gamble. He is not married and would love to have you as a roommate; that way you guys can share the bills."

I looked at them both and said, "I will not be comfortable living with a man as a roommate." I stood up and said, "Thank you." And as I got up from there, I said, "Lord, if I live past this day, I will live to see many more days."

I went into the room I shared with Tutu and the other 3 children, went down on my knees, what I had not done in a long time, and I said, "God, help me; I cannot take this any more. Why is my life so hard; what have I done? Why am I being rejected? What is going on? Look upon me with mercy and protect me. Where do I go from here?" and I wept. The following morning, I made sure the man of the house had gone to work and his wife (at the time was going to a community college) had left for school and the children also had left for school. And as I went outside to sit on the porch, an old green Corvette pulled up to the driveway. As I raised my head up, it was Angela, our neighbor from Makurdi. She lived about a block away from my father's house. She looked at me and said, "Onyeje, what are you doing here?"

I ran into her arms and gave her a big hug. She said, "The last time I saw you was 3 years ago. How is Ihotu?"

I said, "She is fine. She is inside watching PBS kids."

She said, "You look frail and thin, you don't look happy, and you look unkept."

I could not tell her all the story, but I just said, "I came to live with this couple about two months ago, and they told me last night we could not live here anymore because they were moving." She said, "Oh, that's okay, everything will be fine. How long have you been here (in the US)?"

I said, "It's been almost 4 months total. I came in March."

She said, "I come and go for business; my husband and children are back home, and I have a beautiful boutique in Abuja. I am about to leave in two days and was wondering if Helen had any message for her family back home?"

I told her, "She was not back from school yet, but I'll let her know you came by."

Angela now said, "I have a friend who lives about ten minutes away from here; she is a very nice lady and has 5 children. She is newly divorced and has a 3-bedroom house. She would love to keep you and Ihotu until you decide if you want to stay in America or go back home." She also said, "Don't let anyone fool you. Most of the stories we all heard about America in Nigeria were mostly lies. It's not an easy journey, and most people come home and lie about what they really did for a living."

She then said, "You have to be legal to work or even go to school." She went on and on, and I hung onto every word she said, but I was thankful that she was even here. I was so thankful that God sent help. If I had been sleeping when she came and didn't see her outside... I wanted to take one day at a time, and for now, all I was concerned for was a place to stay; I'd worry about the legal part when I got there.

She called the lady on the phone, and her name happened to be Helena. She said it was fine to keep me and Ihotu. When Angela hung up the phone, and told me the lady said it was okay, and to let me have her number, I jumped up and was very excited. It wasn't long before Angela left.

I called Helena and talked with her over the phone. She asked when I was ready to come. I told her I was ready anytime.

The next day was great. I got my bags packed, and a little beam of light started to set in. When the couple arrived, they where shocked to see that I was a little lighter. I greeted them with excitement, and after they had finished dinner, I told them I had great news for them. And when they asked what it was, I said, "Angela came by this afternoon to gather messages to take home for you for your family, and she happened to be my older sister's friend and neighbor from back home. She asked her friend Helena to keep me and Tutu, and Helena agreed, so we are leaving tomorrow."

They both looked at themselves and said, "You should have told us. We thought you would leave when we started moving to the new house. The contractors have only two months to go."

I said, "Thank you so much; you both have done a lot for me already. We will leave tomorrow." I later discovered that Helen and Helena were friends, but the relationship was borderline competitive, and they always wanted to outdo each other. Anyway, at that moment, it was working for me.

It was 9 a.m. in the morning when Helena announced herself. She came to pick Tutu and me up as she said she would. She was very pleseant; she asked me my name and I told her who I was, and she said, "O my Goodness, I know your family and I know your father. Why didn't you tell me you were here?" She picked up my stuff fast, and we were gone. We arrived at her house, and she had cooked Jollof rice for Tutu and I. She called my aunty in Canada and told her I was with her, and she was going to take care of me the best she could.

I was comfortable, and as the weeks went by, she asked me if I knew how to do anything beside the school training I had from the university. I told her I learned how to braid hair a few months ago, and I could clean. I told her I had been home and indoors for a few months and it was getting boring.

That summer, Tutu turned three and was beginning to make sentences and become independent.

It was very hard for me financially. I was an adult making no income and dependent on Helena. She was already working two-and-a-half jobs, with 5 children, no child support, and divorced. I was a visitor and didn't qualify for any government assistance, not like I knew how that was done. Helena told me, "In America, if you live below the poverty line, you could get WIC. The government will give you cheese, bread, cereal and a bread voucher every two weeks." A whole bunch of Nigerians used that to supplement their incomes. Most of the people who lived in the community at the time worked in factories, gas stations, and grocery stores and went to school at night to get a degree so they could climb above the poverty rate. Some did and some didn't. Helena took me around and showed me the ghetto areas as well, and to my surprise I saw Nigerians among the community in the ghetto; they spoke the American accent to the T, had the American swag, and lived in denial.

With horror, I said I'd go back home to Nigeria first before I became a statistic. Maybe the bigger cities had it differently, but this was what my experience was at the time.

The Nigerian community would gather together to celebrate a chid's birthday or wedding ceremony; they wore their traditional clothes and cooked Nigerian food. It was a place for most of them to network; as they celebrated they lamented on how difficult it had been for them to obtain citizenship. Some had not been home in 20 years and with others, 15 was the average or 10, and as I heard these stories I was in shock. Some of them moved from one state to another, and as desperation started to set in, some started getting in trouble with the law. I didn't realize how many Nigerians were locked up and in jail in the US. Greener pastures, some called it, or the American dream had become a nightmare. So many were too ashamed to go back home.

I met a man who told me he was a commissioner back home; he was well paid by the government. He won the visa lottery, sold his house and property, bought a ticket and came to America. For seven years he worked in a nonskilled assembly-line factory, inspecting parts for defects. He was so sad, but he was 8 years into it and had the hope of turning things around. He was 46 at the time. And as I pondered on these people's dilemma, I didn't want to end up the same way. A lot of them had overstayed and become illegal immigrants floating through the system. They jumped anytime the cops drove by or were glued to the TV to hear the latest news on immigration reform; nothing changed from year to year.

PART III: MY VICTORY

Chapter 16: Meeting Segun

Helena thought it would be a great idea to introduce me to some of her friends who needed any little labor done here or there without my illegally working. I went with her to the gas station one day on Highland Road, and the manager of the store happened to know her, and as they chatted, and she pumped her gas, I looked around the interior of the gas station and saw a name on the door, "Employee of the Month: Segun." I looked at the name, and for some reason I asked the manager who that was, and he said, "Oh, it's one of our employees; he goes to school and works when he gets off school in the evening. Does the name strike a bell?"

I said "No, I was just wondering."

Helena told the manager, "She can help you clean out the freezer. Find her something to do; she is bored sitting at home."

He said, "I'll let you know if she can help me here or if my wife will need her to help at home."

As we drove back home, Helena said she would introduce me to the Nigerian community and slowly but surely things will begin to take shape.

I said, "Okay." It wasn't long before the store manager had called to ask Helena if I could come in and watch someone clean the freezer, and if I could do it, he could have me come in and clean it out once a week. I couldn't make it the first time in the morning because Helena had to go to work. When she got back later that afternoon, it was about 6 p.m. when she dropped me off. When I got into the store, a thin, tall, dark-skinned man said hello to us from the glass barrier. He said, "Aunty, good afternoon."

Helena said, "Good afternoon, Segun, how are you? This is my sister from Nigeria; her name is Onyeje. You have to teach her how to clean out the freezer."

He said, "Yes, maam, no problem."

After Helena left, I sat down on the single chair in the shop, and Segun said, "I already cleaned out the freezers today; maybe next time I'll show you how. It's very cold in there; I am not sure you will like it in there."

I said, "Okay, thank you." Somehow it felt like I had met this person before. We just talked, and when customers walked in he moved from the glass barrier, so he could work. His shift went by quickly, and Helena came back to pick me up. As we talked in the car, she asked if I had learned how to clean the freezers, but I told her no, because Segun had already cleaned them. We drove silently back home.

It was September 11th, 2001 when 9/11 happened. I was in the little store where Segun worked; he wasn't working that morning, but I went out there to buy a few things. Everyone was in tumult when the news hit; everything in the gas station came to a standstill so people could hear what was going on. It was that same evening that Helena came home and told me it was not even a good idea for me to go out learning to clean freezers at the gas station. She said that with what had just happened, the immigrant community would be the worst hit, and the best thing to do was to stay away from breaking the law by working illegally.

By this time, I had been in America for 6 months and still was not quite sure of what I was doing and what I wanted to do. I know I wasn't going back to Nigeria. I was living one day at a time. I had no money, I had nothing. Spiritually, I was not connected to anyone or anything. I was hanging on to what I knew from home. I was absorbed into thinking how to make it in America.

Helena and her children went to St. Mary's, a Catholic church by the corner. I got very bored with the mass and rosaries. I had given all that up before I came to America. I had no one to take me to church. Helena was coming out of a bitter divorce, and the last thing she wanted to hear was a church sermon, so we all just lived our own lives. However, I realized a yearning in my heart for God. I would pick up my Bible and read and pray with Ihotu at night.

Our first Christmas had gone by. I was able to call my dad back home in Nigeria. I told him I was doing fine, but I never told him all that I had to go through. He advised me like a dad would do and always ended it with, "Always honor and respect yourself in all that you do."

A few months passed, and as spring came by, I was braiding Tutu's hair outside under the tree in front of Helena's house. A car pulled up with 3 young guys in it; one of them was Helena's son Ali, one was Segun, and another was named Wale. Helena's son waved at me and said to Segun, "Come meet my aunty from Nigeria, and her daughter Ihotu." Up until that point Segun did not know I had a daughter; he didn't know anything about me. And I was uncomfortable with the announcement because I didn't know what to make of the situation. He said, "Hello, Onyeje," and then he turned to Helena's son and said to him, "We met at the gas station a few months back."

I said, "Hi," in a low, unexcited voice, but Tutu ran up and gave him a big hug, and he picked her up. And for a moment I thought to myself, *Okay.*

He stayed outside with us for a while after everyone had gone inside. We didn't have anything to talk about. It was a little awkward.

"What are you doing on Sunday?" Segun asked.

"I don't have any plans; most Sundays I stay home with Tutu. I haven't found any churches around here that I can go to, and to complicate matters I don't drive or have a car.

"I gave my life to Christ shortly before I traveled, but for the first few months I went to Living Faith (Winners' Chapel), and went to a women's fellowship, House of Mercy, at mid-week."

"So how do you keep yourself going spiritually?" he asked.

"For the last few weeks and months, I read my Bible and pray every day. I found a Christian TV channel that shows church services on Sunday, and I tune in and listen to one or two, and that's all. I really do miss going to church."

"That's good! I have been going to a non-denominational church on Fairfax Road for about a year, and the people have been very supportive and treat me like family. Most Sundays after church, I go with the guys or visit with a family and have lunch; that has really helped me. I was going to Redeem Christian Church in Nigeria. It would be nice if you and Tutu would come with me to church on Sunday, if you wouldn't mind. You can think about it, and if you decide to go, please let me know; I will come get you and Tutu on Sunday morning. This is my cell phone number."

I took his number and placed it in my pocket. On second thought I said, "I'll go to church with you."

"That's great! I'll come by at nine in the morning."

It wasn't long after he left that I realized I didn't even have decent clothes to wear to church. I called him up and canceled, telling him we couldn't go till the next time when the weather was warmer. I had

211

two ankara dresses that I brought from Nigeria that could be worn to church, but not in the cold weather.

Time came and went, and we finally went to church with Segun. At this point, Segun had not asked or shown any interest, and I wasn't looking for anything from him. He seemed like a nice young man who was helping me and my daughter. He offered to take me to the grocery store, but I would refuse.

He introduced me to Mrs. Kamson at the church. She took a liking to me and Tutu and almost immediately wanted to adopt Tutu as her own. She would come by after work and pick Tutu up. She bought Tutu her first Barbie doll. Then came the beautiful dresses and a teddy bear. When Tutu turned four years old, she had a birthday party for her at McDonald's with all the little children at church. It wasn't long before my mind kicked in, thinking, *how can I pay all these people back; why are they so kind to me?* I didn't want to enjoy this before it all got taken away, then I started withdrawing.

This church became our regular church every Sunday. Mrs. Kamson would come pick Tutu and me up when Segun could not come. We started meeting people at the church; it was an all-Black congregation. They sang Kirk Franklin songs in their choir for praise and worship, with a mix of the Mississippi mass-choir style. Most people met after church to eat, and it seems like "food" was a never-ending practice in America. Everything revolved around food, from birth to death. We ate all the time.

During the weekdays when Tutu and I had nothing to do, we would go to the public library on Lee Street. Adjacent from the library was the community center. It was not a very good neighborhood. We would go in the building and watch people play basketball or swim; it was a recreation center. Tutu and I loved going there about 2 times a week.

It wasn't long before I saw a group of people singing, and I asked if I could watch. One day while we sat down listening, the choir director asked if I wanted to join. I told him I wasn't sure if I could sing, but he said, "Come over here and sing Amazing Grace, and I'll let you know if you can sing or not."

I said, "Okay," and as I started singing.

He raised his hand and said, "Young lady, get in the third row; you're a rich alto. We can use that voice up in here!"

I became a part of the community choir and we would practice different songs. We sang difficult songs like the Fisk Jubilie Choir choruses; it was an acappella style of singing.

Not long after I joined the choir, Marvin Sapp was coming to Greensboro for a concert, and the leader of the group was asked to have us sing his back up. I thought that was cool. It was on a Saturday evening, so I went with Segun and Tutu, and I really enjoyed myself.

We met Mr. Osborne at the church, who was a handyman, and he introduced me to one of his clients, Mrs. Whitefields, who lived in a beautiful home in Lake Jeanette, a highbrow area in Greensboro. She was an artist and a painter and needed some painting work done. I had never painted before, but I was determined to learn and work, so when she asked me if I could paint, I said "Most certainly."

She came out to pick me up in the morning to her home, and as she painted (as an artist), I mixed buckets of paint and painted her walls and her garage, but first I laid blue tape all around the edges, then I painted the first layer and then applied the second coat. I did quite an impressive job, and at the end of the day Mrs. Whitefields gave me $40; I was excited. I had paint in my hair, on my face and on my nails, but my life had gradually changed and I was doing the hard labor.

After a while, we became friends and she treated me nice. She introduced me to Once Upon a Child, a gently used children's clothing store, with children's toys and so many useful items. I went to the store, and with $20 I was able to buy Tutu a new pair of shoes, some dresses and toys. Each day, I would spend about 4 or 5 hours painting; she'd drop us off after the end of each day. When I wasn't painting, I cleaned and washed her bathrooms and did other housework. While I painted, Tutu sat in the living room watching PBS Kids. I painted for Mrs. Whitefields until all her rooms and interiors were done.

For Tutu's birthday that year she bought her many toys and clothes. I did whatever my hands found to do, and before long I was fixing every lady's hair at the church including my pastor's wife. I would go to my pastor's house on Saturdays and clean. I started helping at the church and answering the phones during the day, and at noon we would gather together at the church office and pray.

On Saturdays, Segun and I with some members of the church would go to the surrounding neighborhoods to evangelize. We went to the rough neighborhoods, knocked on people's doors, passed out flyers, and prayed along with people. It was something I looked forward to every weekend.

Mrs. Kamson would talk to me all the time and encourage me to give life a chance. Although I was beginning to live a little, I had my walls and was ready to crush anything that came my way. I had no soft spot left in me; I was wired for survival. All anyone got from me on a personal level was a smile. I didn't hug anyone, I didn't look at anyone in the eye, and I read in between the lines when I listened to any conversation. I was quick to call it a day when I sensed anything that looked like control or manipulation. I was very bold and wasn't afraid to tell you my honest opinion even though it hurt.

While I was talking to Mrs. Kamson one day, Segun came by to visit her and asked me if I would go to lunch with him, and I could bring Tutu along. I said "No"; I didn't even consider it.

Two weeks went by when he asked again. This time, Mrs. Kamson said, "Onyeje, it's okay; just go. I'll come with you and Tutu; let me pay for it if you feel uncomfortable with Segun paying."

When Segun left, I told Mrs. Kamson that I didn't want to feel indebted to anyone, and I didn't know why she was so kind to me. I told her, "I have nothing in America, and I cannot repay anyone back for anything." She laughed and said to me, "My daughter, relax."

I took a day to think about the lunch outing and figured it wasn't a bad idea after all, so I told Mrs. Kamson that I would like to go to lunch if she still wanted to be there with Tutu and I.

She said, "Sure," and asked me if I had a way of communicating with Segun. I told her he gave me his number, so l went into the room and called him to let him know I would like to go to lunch.

The day for lunch came, we got ready and Segun picked us up. We went to a Chinese buffet; there was so much food that I lost my appetitie; I couldn't eat. I just kept picking on my food. As the silence grew, Tutu looked up to Segun and said to him, "Can I call you Daddy"?

Segun said, "Yes, sure."

I prayed, *O Lord, open this ground let me fall inside and cover me.* If a black person could turn pale or white, I was beyond white. I was shocked. Mrs. Kamson tried to break the awkward moment, but the damage was already done. Tutu was only 4 years old and she continued eating and giggling, but I had had enough, and it was time to go.

I'll bet Segun was wondering why this young lady was so guarded. That same night, I came home and went to my room. I knelt down beside the bed and talked to God like I never did before. I said, "Lord, this young man is around me for a reason; please help me. He doesn't know me or my story; I don't want to be hurt again. I am tired of crying; I don't want to cry for Paul anymore. This is too much for my heart to handle. See what happened in the restaurant? How do I explain what Tutu did? I am embarrassed before this young man. What do I tell him if he asks me about my past?" I was so ashamed and wanted my past to disappear. And as I talked to God, I cried and went to sleep.

I woke up the next day with some sense of peace. I needed answers. Time was beginning to go by quickly, as I had one more year left on my visa. I was tired; America was not what I thought it to be. I said to myself, *Fine, I made a mistake, at least I tried.* It was time to go back home to my father and just accept what my portion in life would be. I had had enough; the life was hard; people worked all the time. I was not productive, and I decided to go back to Nigeria. I didn't tell anyone because I didn't want anyone to talk me out of it. I got everything ready. *I know how to call the yellow cab, I'll write a little note to everyone to thank them and then take my return ticket and passport and leave. No one will miss me,* I said. *I won't have to be a burden to anyone. At least at home my father could give me a life where I didn't have to suffer like this; this was not living,* I thought to myself; *this was low life. I was a college graduate and was hiding in*

217

the trenches, and I kept on on and on and on; I had a plan. Little did I know that my world was going to take another turn.

As I was planning these things in my heart over the weeks and months, because I started going back to church, I began to communicate with God more often: I would read my Bible, and I would pray as well. As I made this plan to go back home, I asked God to help me because I was no longer able to continue with the hardship. Tutu would turn five in a little while; she had not even started school. I didn't know what to do, and no one had the right information.

But God had a plan for me. I decided it would be unfair to leave without telling Segun, so I called him, and he came by as I sat in the living room in Helena's house. I told him I had decided to go back to Nigeria; I told him all my reasons and that it would be best if I left. I thanked him for how kind he had been to us, and that it wasn't fair for me not to let him know that I was leaving. He kept quiet for a while until the silence became awkward. Then I said, "Did you hear what I just said?"

He said, "Yes I did, but what if I tell you not to go, because since the first day I met you I liked you, and something in me told me you will be my wife."

I laughed and said, "You don't know me, and you don't even know my story. How about you wait and let me tell you about my life, and then see if you want all of it."

That was the first time I ever told him I was a widow and that 5 years ago I had married, and death had snatched my husband away. I told him how I was grieving before I came to America, and just the chaos of being here had not allowed me to think properly. I told him about my encounter in Atlanta. I told him how I was only legally supposed to be here for 2 years, and I didn't want to end up like so many other people. I didn't want to hide, and I didn't want to live like a servant. In my father's house I could eat what I wanted and wear what I wanted; I grew up having anything I wanted: house helps, cooks, drivers and private teachers. I told him the transition was too much of a shock and I could not handle it anymore. I told him I was only trying it out to prove a point to my dad that I was grown up and could handle myself, but I was wrong! I told him it was risky for me staying here, and I was not built to wing life. I told him the only reason I made it this year and some weeks in America was the sparkle in my daughter's eyes, and if I didn't have her, I probably would not be alive. I told him the healing process for me was taking longer than I thought, and my emotions and feelings were shot up.

He didn't let me continue. He took my hands and said, "Let us pray." I bet he saw something in me that I could not see; he saw the pain and the grief, and whatever else he saw, God helped him. He said, "I do really care for you."

I said, "You're working in a gas station and going to university; you can't take care of me. It will be too much of a burden on you. And

219

what if your mother objects? I really don't have a lot of room in my heart for disappointments."

He said in a very calm voice, "I can work two jobs, and I will take care of you and our daughter. My mother will love you, and if she objects, which I know she won't, I have chosen you."

So, I said, "Okay."

Chapter 17: Remarried

It wasn't long before I told Mrs. Kamson that Segun had asked for a date, and I had said "Yes."

She was very excited for me, and I felt a sense of peace in my heart when I agreed to be patient for a while. It wasn't long before Helena picked up on the vibe. She said, "Did that small boy ask you out?"

I said, "Yes."

She smiled and said, "Okay." I am not sure what that meant at that time.

Not long after the Nigerian community found out that Segun and I started dating, everything was done to break us up. They told him how stupid he was and came back to tell me how ignorant I was and that nobody had done this in America. They insisted that I just got here and was rushing to marry someone that could not care for me.

One Saturday morning, Segun called his mom and told her he found a girl he wanted to marry. They spoke in Yoruba and English, back and forth, and then his mom asked to speak to me. She was very pleasant on the phone and asked me who my parents were and how I met her son. I answered her questions and she said she was happy to talk to me over the phone. After the conversation, Segun knew that he had his mom's and dad's blessing.

I called my dad to tell him I had met a man I wanted to marry. He was not so sure he heard me correctly. After long hours on the phone convincing him, he requested to talk to Segun over the phone. My dad wanted to know his background and wanted to know about his family and where he came from. It took several phone calls to finally calm him down; it was his care for me and the pain I had gone through that my dad wanted to be sure of, and that I wasn't making a decision out of loneliness. I convinced my dad I was comfortable and wasn't afraid. I told my dad he was gentle and soft–spoken, and he cared for me and Tutu.

Back home in Nigeria, Segun's parents called my dad and decided to travel from Lagos to Makurdi to officially meet my parents. The formal introduction was done six months later, and both families met and celebrated our union. My soon-to-be mother-in-law was not shy with words as she won my father's heart; they struck up a long family friendship.

Segun talked to the pastor of the church we both attended. He was pleased that we had come to him and asked us to go through marriage counseling for three months before he married us. While Segun went to school full time, he worked at the convinence store full time. On Saturdays we went to counseling for about 2 hours, going through a workbook; premarital counseling was great, but it didn't include the most important things in the marriage—when marriage became tough and life became hard, the lessons in marriage counseling were nowhere to be found; they did not apply to my situation; I could not

222

remember a thing; it did not teach me what to expect as a wife and a mother; it taught me the needs of a man and the needs of a woman, but then I realized that my needs and Segun's needs were not in the manual. Based on the different cultural backgrounds, there was no counseling that reconciled our differences. Marriage counseling did nothing because we had needs ouside of the counseling manual that only God could fulfill.

Three months went by so fast. I had no money, and now we had to prepare for a wedding. Segun and I had to honor God and do the right thing. So many people around us told us to just live together for a while and have the wedding later—it was America, and no one really cared. We insisted we didn't want to do that, so we decided to have a wedding anyway. The wedding date was set for April.

By this time Hope, one of the ladies at the church, had become close friends with me, and she would come over to visit me and I would visit her, and we became close friends. She started helping me plan the wedding. She was very good with her hands, so we went out to the paper company and bought some cardboard and made wedding invitations. She asked her friends Rosline, Theresa, and Angela to help organize the wedding. I didn't work, so I had much time on my hands.

One day when all the girls gathered, I asked all four of them if they wanted to be in my wedding as bridesmaids; they all were excited and said yes. The following day we all went to David's Bridal looking for dresses. I chose my favorite colors, burgundy and gold. And I asked the girls to choose whatever style they wanted. I had not bought my wedding gown yet and wasn't sure how I was going to pay for one.

Two days later, I was watching the local news and a commercial for David's Bridal was on TV for the ninety-nine-dollar wedding-gown sale. I was so excited that I went out the next day. I took Tutu along with me. We looked at so many gowns, then gradually made it to the $99-dress aisle. I didn't go to the store with any style in mind. But then I saw a simple spaghetti-strap gown with a tulle skirt; it was a princess-style dress. I picked it up, wore it, and as I looked at myself in the mirrow, I started to cry. The ladies in the store all looked and said, "You look beautiful in that gown; you should get it." And Tutu looked up at me and said, "Mommy, you look pretty in this dress." At this time, Tutu was 4 years old and would be turning 5 in May.

So many emotions ran through my heart. What I saw in the mirrow was a broken woman, a woman that had been hurt, and a woman that had scars from disappointments. I wanted to wish all that away, but then I was afraid I would not be a happy bride for Segun, and he deserved to be happy. I had too much heaviness on me, but then again, I said to myself, *It's too late now, I'll just go ahead with the wedding.* I took off the dress and called Segun. I told him I'd found a dress at the bridal store.

He said, "Do you like it?"

I said, "Yes."

He said, "You don't sound excited."

I said, "Yes, I am."

But then he said, "Wait there; I'll be on my way." He hung up the phone and in 15 minutes he was at the store. He asked me again if I liked the dress, and I said yes. He asked the lady up front, she told him how much it was, and he paid for it. Immediately something in my heart changed. I knew right then God had given me a kind man, and I was going to go on this journey called life with him. The process was going to be long, but I was confident I had my cheerleader with me.

Three weeks before the wedding, I started developing cold feet. I wasn't sure I wanted to go through with the wedding. I started to ponder in my heart and ask questions: *What if something happens to him, what will I do? I don't want to lose another husband.* Right in the middle of those thoughts, the words Mommy Aluma had spoken to me right before I left Nigeria came back to my heart that God was going to "bless me with a young husband" and "that we will live together until we were tired of living." Those words flooded my spirit, and as I remembered them, I began to cry, and then I asked the Lord to heal my heart, heal my hurt, remove the doubts, and build me up. I told God I could not go through this journey by myself; I had no manual for life expectations and I needed guidance. I needed Him to hold my hands and walk me through life. I needed Him to teach me to be a whole woman, a wife, a mother, a sister and a friend. I didn't know how to do all this stuff. I asked God why my life was so different. After I talked to God, I knew He was going to help me, and the healing process began.

We sent out the cards, I called my sisters back home, and they were all excited for me. My brother Ofu, who was at the University of Maine at Machias at the time, became one of Segun's groomsmen. Dupe, Segun's older sister who lived in London, attended the wedding. We had talked over the phone so many times, and I was going to meet her for the first time. His best man was his childhood friend who came from London. Jennifer came from Atlanta and did my makeup; she was a Mary Kay consultant and a big sister to me at the time. Everyone was so gracious. I extended an invitation to Amos, the man who had driven Tutu and me to the Greyhound bus stop to move from Atlanta to Greensboro. He was in tears all through the wedding ceremony. My aunty Felicia came from Ontario, Canada. The morning of the wedding, we were arranged in the small church on Fairfax Road in Greensboro. Segun and I did not want the traditional "Here Comes the Bride" song, so we picked "The Prayer of Jabez" as our entry song. The community choir I had spent time with on weekdays at Lee Street Community Center, sang the song "Beautiful," and until this day, that song has been my favorite. Words alone could not describe what was going on in that church room that day. Pastor Richard Johnson kept us standing for three hours, preaching a marriage sermon. My knees were shaking, and Tutu began to cry and fuss; she was my little bride. At the 3.5-hour mark,

226

the wedding vows were taken, and when the minister said, "You may now kiss the bride," I was too shy, and I turned my face to the side, and everyone in the church started to laugh; that was the highlight of my wedding! I don't like public affection, and I was not about to start on my wedding day. And who said kissing the bride and smudging red lipstick on the groom made for a long-lasting marriage anyway? Just saying!

We had a beautiful wedding. The food was amazing. Mrs. Kamson and Aunty Mercy, Dupe, and the other ladies had spent time cooking Nigerian food, Jollof rice, chicken, meat pie, and Moi Moi. Aunty Helena made Fufu and pounded yam. The ladies at the church had made traditional American dishes, and we had much food and much left over. I had my wedding cake baked by Judy Daniels; she was a talented woman who was an attorney at the time but loved baking. She made the best red velvet cake, and that was what she made for me on my wedding and charged me nothing for it. The wedding reception went on until about 7 p.m., then Segun and I left the crowd.

It was funny because the next day we came to church in the morning, but little did we know that it was daylight savings, and the time had moved forward, so we came in an hour after church had started. As we walked in, the minister stopped the service to announce the new couple, and the whole church laughed in joy and laughed some more, because we were so surprised why they where laughing so much. Later we found out we had come in an hour late, and for some reason it was funny. In America, I guess to have a couple come to church the day after their wedding was odd when we were supposed to be on our honeymoon.

A few weeks after my wedding, my phone rang, and it was an Atlanta caller ID. I picked up the phone, and it was Uche's friend, Lisa's husband. He said "Please don't hang up the phone. Amos told me he was at your wedding and he gave me your number. I have been trying to reach you. In the last 2 years, my wife Lisa died of diabetic complications, but the reason for my call is to say that I am very sorry for all that I did to you; I did not stand for you or protect you from my friend Uche. I am very sorry; please forgive me." The silence on the phone was so awkward I didn't know what to say, I told him I was sorry about his wife passing. Whatever else I said to him I cannot remember, but I told him I had moved on by the grace of God and didn't want anyone calling me.

By Monday, Segun, Tutu and I moved to a 2-bedroom, one-bath apartment, and that would become our home for the next seven years.

Chapter 18: Healing Process

Segun went back to school almost immediately after our wedding. He was an Electrical Engineering student at the university and had one more year to complete his schooling. He also continued to work full time. I could not work because I was not on a work visa, so I would spend most of my mornings cleaning the apartment, cooking, and going out to the library and the park with Tutu.

She had reached school age and started elementary school, so I was left at home by myself everyday until about 3 p.m. I had so much time on my hands, I bought a violin and started taking lessons. But it wasn't too long before I knew I could not keep up with the expense of taking private lessons, so I packed that up.

I started spending time reading my Bible, praying and praising God. I did that for many weeks, and as I continued I noticed that my joy was beginning to return. I was beginning to get excited about life again.

It wasn't long afterwards that I went to the library one day, and as I was talking to a lady, she asked me if I was interested in going back to school. I told her that I was, and she took me to Guilford Technical Community College (GTCC) and introduced me to a guidance counselor. We talked about different career pathways and how I could start taking classes. I told her what education I had from Nigeria, but that I had always loved to care for people. I told her I loved to communicate passionately and would like to be able to become an advocate. She said, "You seem to be a caring person. Have you ever thought of becoming a nurse? You can accomplish your goals if you go to nursing school. You can always branch out into different areas, because nursing is very diverse."

I told her up front that I would be interested in starting the program, and she asked to see if I could have my transcript sent from Nigeria. At the time, communication and the Internet were nothing like now. It was so hard getting any information across. I called my father and told him I was going to go back to school. He was pleased and said he would do anything he could to send my transcript over. The transcript started taking longer than it should have, and one month became 6 months and then one year, so I decided to start from scratch and sat for the GED exams. Then I tested out of some of the math and other prerequisite classes. I could not afford to go into a traditional class setting, so I figured that testing out of the prerequisites would leave me with only nursing major classes. While I was taking classes at the community college, I discovered I was pregnant with Joshua. Life was about to get hard, like it wasn't hard enough.

Segun was already stretched to the max; all we did was pay our rent and a few bills, and now I was pregnant and in school. I told myself at least I didn't have to worry for the next 9 months until the baby was born. I spent more time studying as much as I could, but nine months came before I knew it, and I had Joshua. His birth was not an easy one, and I almost lost him at the time of delivery. My amniotic fluid had leaked out, and for days I was walking around with no fluid in my womb. As my belly got heavier, I was uncomfortable and went to the hospital after taking a test in the morning. After the doctor had assessed me and looked at the ultrasound, he said he would not let me go home because my baby was in distress, and I needed to be induced immediately.

Ihotu had a baby brother now; she was 6 years older. She adored Joshua and wanted to pick him up all the time. I had to keep my eyes on him 24/7, because Tutu wanted to play with him like one of her doll babies. Joshua came into our lives with so much joy; he was a quiet and contented baby. Segun was a father for the first time, and we were now both twenty-nine. I was going to meet my mother-in-law for the first time, six weeks after Joshua was born. Segun's mother came from Nigeria to spend some time with us. It was much-needed help. Although my child-bearing experience was better in America, I had no family around me; I had no one to give me hot baths and massage my belly with hot towels. So, when Segun's mom came, she kept the baby, so I could get some sleep. We bonded well, and she went back home to Nigeria after a while.

At this time, I had completed all my prerequisites, but could not apply to the nursing program because I had just had a baby, so I had to wait for another 2 years. I couldn't go out as much. Segun and I had an old jaloppy that had only one door on the passenger's side that would open. We had to cross over to the other side to get to the driver's side to drive. My routine had changed since I could no longer drop him off and pick him up after school and work, so I stayed home. Our finances got very tight, and somedays we would pray for money, and pray for our daily needs. God was faithful; we never went to bed hungry. We experienced countless miracles. There were times when people would knock on our door and bring a bag of groceries and say, "I just felt in my heart to bring you guys some groceries." And as soon as I closed the door, I would dance and thank God for answering our prayers.

My pantry was empty, and we were living from paycheck to paycheck. It got so bad that, one year we were behind on our rent for three months; when Ellen Johnson had come to visit us, she wanted me to do her hair, and when I did, she went home and came back and gave me the money to cover our three months' rent!

Segun and I started to look inward to see what we could do differently. We were going through a process and didn't know any better. My immigration papers had been filed and were being reviewed, and we could not expedite the process; all we had to do was wait. Looking back, I was not physically sick, and none of the children were sick. God kept us from year to year. Segun did not show any signs that he was tired or stressed, but I noticed he was doing a lot of thinking at night, and I started feeling guilty. But we were able to talk over things together. One thing he said that encouraged me was that he never regretted his decision, and things were going to get better.

I picked myself up and continued to read my Bible and spent a lot of time praising God. I would play a praise CD and dance myself happy.

Segun and I would gather a couple of our close friends on Fridays and we would pray all night and share God's Word and encourage one another. We all talked about our dreams and found consolation in how our lives would change in the future in our little apartment. We did that for years. None of us at the time was living the so-called American dream; we didn't even know what that looked like. Every one of us in that circle was going through hard times. We all had to make up our minds to either stand with God and wait for His deliverance, or take the other way and make things happen and pay the consequences. We all knew better; we had come too far to compromise.

Segun and I would have our little disagreements. He was not the one to talk a lot, and that would add to my irritations because I was a communicator and wanted to know what we should do next. Things were not moving fast enough, so I started to get impatient. He was very calm, and the opposite of me. I would look at him and wonder, *"There must be something more to this guy; maybe I'll find out later,"* but it was nothing but my old mind creeping in to cause trouble. I took everything to God. Slowly but surely, Segun and I realized that we had to keep our mind in a place of speaking God's Word and believing everything He said. Even though we were tithers, at the time we had allowed fear of our future and the present hardship to cripple us. We would speak God's Word one day and speak fear the next. Soon we realized we had to make a conscious decision to stick with the program, or there was no way out. We pulled out our Bibles and began

233

writing Scriptures out and sticking them all over the house. I remember Segun's favorite Scripture he placed by his bedside:

Philippians 4:6–7 (NKJV): Be anxious for nothing, but in everything by prayer and supplication, with thanksgiving, let your requests be made known to God; and the peace of God, which surpasses all understanding, will guard your hearts and minds through Christ Jesus.

And on the refrigerator, we stuck:

Philippians 4:19 (KJV): But my God shall supply all your needs according to his riches in glory by Christ Jesus.

And as we looked over these Scriptures, we spoke them out loud every day, and we became accountable to each other. We promised not to say anything negative about our situation and to rejoice knowing that God would open every door. We then decided to put a Scripture on the wall right by the telephone, so when the phone rang, it was the first thing we'd see when we answered, and it reminded us what to focus on:

Philippians 4:8 (KJV): Finally, brethren, whatsoever things are true, whatsoever things are honest, whatsoever things are just, whatsoever things are pure, whatsoever things are lovely, whatsoever things are of good report; if there be any virtue, and if there be any praise, think on these things.

We wanted our conversation to honor God and honor people, so we started taking baby steps and, slowly but surely, we began to see what the Word of God said concerning us. America is a place where it is easy to forget and get entangled in the rat race, so many believers who came to America especially from Nigeria, trusting in God, fell through the cracks when the pressures of America kicked in, when challenges came, and when America revealed what it had in store for non-citizens and immigrants who had no clue. It was not the glitze and glamour. America was not for the lazy and undisciplined. It was not for the faint of heart. The compromises stared you in the face, day in and day out, and it was a choice to win or give up. It was sad to hear how some of these people would say, "This is America, now"; and "Church don't pay your bills"; and that "God will bless your hustle"; really? The mindset was wrong and Segun and I had to start digging deeper. We loved the Lord, but we had no proper guidance, so we started searching on our own. We didn't want to be defeated and in bondage, proclaiming victory in disguise. We started listening to papa David Oyedekpo and Pastor Paul Enenche; we started praying and following the principles we were taught, and things began to turn around. We grabbed a hold of Kenneth Copland's tapes and Papa Kenneth Hagin's faith messages, and our confidence began to change, and hope started to rise. We saturated our environment and believed for a different outcome. When we gave, we knew that God was going to bless our seed. We spoke God's Word over every seed and expected a return. And not long after that, we started getting calls from Immigration, and my paperwork began to get worked upon. I

235

received a Social Security card in the mail, and with that I was able to obtain a certified nursing assistant license. I got a part-time job and started working a few hours a week.

We had made friends with some neighbors, and one lady said, "I can keep your son during the day while you take classes, and you can keep my son while I go to work in the afternoon." That was an answered prayer, so I started applying for a spot in the Nursing program. I was denied a spot the first time I tried. It was a hard program to get into, as they had a very limited number of seats. I didn't give up this time. Joshua was almost 2 years old. And the following year in the spring I tried again, and I was accepted into the Nursing program at the community college.

I started school with the determination of completing school in 2 years, and things looked bright, but after the first semester, I became pregnant with my third child, Josiah. I knew I wasn't going to quit. I knew it was my one chance at school again, so I gave it my all, but close to my ninth month mark, I started to have difficulty with the pregnancy. The baby would not come at the time he was due. I talked to the department chair of my nursing program, and she advised me to quit school and reapply. I told her I couldn't do that unless she promised I could come back to join from where I had stopped. She said she could not promise that, and it would be my choice to leave the program. She wished me luck and said to keep my fingers crossed; all I needed to pass was a 75%. I walked out of her office and wished for the best. I came home and told Segun about my discussion with the department chair. He said, "Everything will work out fine."

I had a test the following day, and after the test the next day, I felt heavy and drove to the women's clinic. On arrival, I told the nurse I was feeling a little heavy and just wanted to get checked. She said okay and sat me up on the bed. She asked me to place my book bag on the side and take off my maternity jeans. The baby was about a week overdue and had not made any effort to come out. She placed me on the ultrasound monitor again and asked me my name and date of birth; when I told her, she said, "Today is your birthday; happy birthday!"

I said thank you. But as she looked at the ultrasound monitor, I noticed her facial expression started changing; the baby's heart rate was fine but weak. She said, "Mem, did you break your water?"

I said, "No, I have never broken my water before, and I remember what happened with my first son, so I didn't want to take chances."

She said, "Well your body has reabsorbed your amniotic fluid, and I can't even see the baby on the monitor. We have to get the baby out as soon as possible so he won't go into distress." She ran out and got the doctor, who checked the monitors and asked me to sign a consent, and immediately gave me pitocin to induce labor.

I couldn't reach my husband because he was working and was not allowed to have his phone on him. Things were a little different at the time, so I called my friend Ann and asked her to pick up Tutu from the school bus and take her home. She came to the hospital and collected my keys and went back to get Tutu. I made one more phone call to Ellen Johnson, who came over to the hospital and stayed with me during the birth of my son.

Nine hours passed and still no contractions. The doctor said he already started to induce me and did not want to give more anesthesia for a Caesarian section. Ellen stood in the room and prayed; as the pain became unbearable, the doctor ordered an epidural to help along the way. The contractions were so heavy, the doctor said he would use forceps to get the baby out. Then I started losing consciousness, and in that moment, it looked like I had an out-of-body experience. I was looking down at my body lying in the bed, and Ellen was pacing back and forth in my hospital room praying. Segun came in and he was praying, but I noticed he was crying, and he was asked to step aside. It happened so quick. And then I heard a voice say "push," and as I did, I heard a baby cry. Josiah was an ounce short of 9 lb. at birth. He came in at 3 a.m., a few hours after my birthday. So, we share the same birth month. Up until this day, no one could explain to me why my body kept reabsorbing my amniotic fluid. I stayed in the hospital, and after 3 days we left to go home.

Even though things had started getting better, we were still in crunch mode, but we were not where we used to be. Segun had just graduated from a four-year college and was applying for jobs while working at a grocery store to put food on the table and pay the bills. I was in school and having my third child. Joshua had just turned three years old when Josiah came on the scene. The previous year I had given away all my baby clothes and crib and was not expecting to have another child until I was done with school. Anyway, we drove to Walmart from the hospital and purchased a basinet and a few baby clothes and went home. But in all of this, God was faithful. We had friends come by to visit and brought in baby clothes and diapers. I had never had a baby shower, but the supplies I received exceeded my expectations.

I had been away from school for five days, and for that program I had only about twenty-four hours of clinical absences allowed. I returned to school the following Thursday morning, because I had a test. Segun had to stay home with the baby, and I was still sore all over. I failed that test; it wasn't funny—the worst exam I ever took in my life. My total class average fell to a 69 and I knew that was it for me. I had one more test to go, and I had to make a 74 or higher to pass or drop out. During all this, I wouldn't lose hope. I came home and knelt beside my bed and asked the Lord to help me like He always did. Then I praised Him and got up. On Sunday morning we had gone to church, and while the message was coming forth that morning, a word had come forth from my pastors that "the stop block had been removed," and as he got out of the pulpit and ran around inside the church, I took off my shoes and ran behind him. It looked foolish, but I had to take a step of faith; that was Sunday morning.

By Monday morning, we were preparing for our final exam. I went to school and took my final exam for the semester. Yes, God helped me. He gave me more than enough points. I graduated nursing school in these two years!

Segun continued to work in the grocery store at night and continued applying and going for interviews for a professional job during the day. He would travel out of state to Boston and Philadelphia for interviews, and some of the jobs offered demanded some compromises that went against his core values. It looked like nothing was happening, but we kept our eyes on the One Who promised to make all things beautiful in His time. So, we prayed together and gave thanks as we asked God for direction and clarity.

Chapter 19: Where I Am Today

In the year 2010, God visited us; all the doors opened in one year. I had graduated and sat for my boards; I passed and got hired within 4 weeks of graduation. A few months after that, the engineering company, where Segun had been working in a temporary positon for a year without the engineering salary and benefits, called him and gave him a full-time position on the spot. In that same year we had moved into our new home in a beautiful side of town—a brand-new five-bedroom brick house. In that same year we bought two cars. And just like a dream, everything changed before our eyes; the doors opened.

In 2011, I returned back to school and obtained a Bachelor's degree in nursing. In 2014, we started a thriving family business. Three years later in 2017 I decided it was time to expand my knowledge and have more autonomy in my area of practice, so I went back to school to obtain a Masters of Science degree as a nurse practitioner. I am a few months away from graduation.

Ihotu is a responsible, beautiful young lady; she is now 20 years old and a junior in college. Joshua is 14 and in high school. Josiah is 11 and starting middle school after this summer. Segun and I are more committed to one another; our love has grown sweeter as the years have gone by. We have met so many wonderful people and established lasting relationships. God has changed me and taught me by Himself. We have come a long way; with the ups and downs and the challenges we faced in America, we have stayed on top, victoriously. God saw us through. We did not have to compromise our stand and force our way through. As I look back and see how God lifted me from the dark place of shame and sorrow to a place of rest and love, a place of restoration. The American dream was not God's dream for me. I wanted God's purpose and dream for my life. I had to seek God's face to give me direction every step of the way. I went from fear and shame to a place of honor and beauty, a place of hurt to forgiveness. I had to turn it all over to God and trust him to heal my wounds. And He did exceedingly abundantly above all that I could have ever asked or imagined (Ephesians 3:20–21).

Mandate

The year 2017 was a turnaround for me spiritually. Prior to that year we had experienced a loss in the family—Segun's dad had passed on. I had gone through some health challenges and multiple motor-vehicle accidents. We started to hunger for a deeper revelation, asking questions about our spiritual growth and purpose in life. There was so much hunger for God's Word and His presence, that as we spent time together as a family, God began to give us specific instructions and directions. Segun decided as a family for us to go to a convention and vacation, so we went to the Southwest Believers Convention 2017. SWBC was a confirmation of our journey into God's purpose for our lives. The experiences, encounters and manifestations at those meetings changed our lives forever. In the month of September of the same year, I had received instructions to go on a fast, and as I waited before the Lord in the place of prayer and praise, He gave me a mandate in Isaiah 61:1–3 (NIV). In the place of prayer, He outlined and gave clear instructions:

The Year of the Lord's Favor

The Spirit of the Sovereign Lord is on me,

because the Lord has anointed me

to proclaim good news to the poor.

He has sent me to bind up the brokenhearted,

to proclaim freedom for the captives

and release from darkness for the prisoners,

to proclaim the year of the Lord's favor

and the day of vengeance of our God,

to comfort all who mourn,

and provide for those who grieve in Zion—

to bestow on them a crown of beauty

243

instead of ashes,

the oil of joy

instead of mourning,

and a garment of praise

instead of a spirit of despair.

They will be called oaks of righteousness,

a planting of the Lord

for the display of his splendor.

And as I pondered on this Scripture, I laid it before the Lord and covered it in prayers, and then the questions started to flood my heart. *How, Lord? I didn't go to Bible school; I am not qualified. I know how to care for people in the health care field, but how do I do this?* And as these questions continued to go through my heart, I remembered the vision I had when I was in Nigeria, a few months after Paul had passed. I traveled with Atokolo and his wife to a ministers' conference, and as I sat in the car sleeping in the hot sun, I saw a woman sitting beside me with her head lying on my shoulder—she was in despair; she was crying. In that vision, I kept comforting her and soothing her. I touched her hair and patted her like a baby with reassurance. Then it didn't make much sense to me, because I was just one year or less from losing a spouse and was still hurting; I was in no place to comfort or console anyone, but now it all made sense, that with the same comfort I received, I would comfort others.

Praise be to the God and Father of our Lord Jesus Christ, the Father of compassion and the God of all comfort, who comforts us in all our troubles, so that we can comfort those in any trouble with the comfort we ourselves receive from God.

2 Corinthians 1:3–4 (NIV)

Then as I continued in the place of prayer, He said, "Out of you shall flow rivers of living water," and I looked it up in the Bible, where it says, *"Whoever believes in me, as Scripture has said, rivers of living water will flow from within them" (John 7:38 NIV)*. I understand this to be a carrier of life and refreshment. And Ezekiel 47:1–12 was impressed in my heart and, opening the Scriptures, it was still talking about the living water but this time on a different level. I basked in His presence.

After the days of waiting before the Lord, I experienced a spiritual shift that words cannot describe: I knew deep within me a change had taken place. Fasting is not changing God—Jesus has already completed the work on Calvary; fasting puts us in a position to hear, receive direction and increase our faith in what we have been praying for. It eliminated the toxic emotions and strife, and empowered us to stand, knowing who we are in Christ. And from that position we always win. That's true spiritual warfare. The peace of God flooded my soul and the joy of the Lord returned in full. So, I set myself up to obey the Lord no matter the cost. I was ready to put everything aside that was dragging and pulling me in the wrong direction. I had to change jobs and disassociate myself with relationships that were not sharpening me but instead were drowning my purpose.

What the Future Holds

As time went by, I asked the Lord to show me how to do all that He had asked me to do. As I kept asking questions, I heard in my heart, "Onyeje, I have not asked you to do anything beyond My grace; all I have asked you to do is tell people your story. Tell them how I delivered you." Then he said, "Why don't you start by completing the book you started five years ago?" I got up from the place of prayer and was encouraged.

God is not asking us for more. He is not a taskmaster, trying to set us up to fail. If He asks of us anything, He will back us up 100%. God wants to show us off as His children. We are the light of the world; we reflect the Father, and His presence in us can accomplish more than we can ever know. The vision will unfold gradually. We must trust Him every step of the way. The challenges will come, but our eyes must be on God.

I have written my story, and shared my journey, and walked you through my victory.

I pray for all who read this book that they will have an encounter with the loving Father. Wait patiently for Him, as the Psalmist wrote in Psalm 40:1–3 (NIV):

> *I waited patiently for the Lord;*
>
> *he turned to me and heard my cry.*
>
> *He lifted me out of the slimy pit,*
>
> *out of the mud and mire;*
>
> *he set my feet on a rock*
>
> *and gave me a firm place to stand.*
>
> *He put a new song in my mouth,*
>
> *a hymn of praise to our God.*
>
> *Many will see and fear the Lord*
>
> *and put their trust in him.*

Do not allow your pain, shame, grief and loss to take over your life. The same God who did it for me will do it for you, too.

Restoration Prayer

Father I have come before You today in the power of the resurrected Jesus whose I am. I stand upon the finished work of Jesus and on the authority of the believer. It is in the validity of the death, burial and resurrection of Jesus that I present my case before You today.

I pray for healing in my emotions, my mind and my soul, from the crown of my head to the soles of my feet. I will not fear, I will not be afraid, I refuse to be humiliated, and I will not be ashamed. I receive healing from the shame of my youth, and I will not remember the reproach and stigma of widowhood any more.

You're my Maker, and my Husband; You're the Lord of Hosts. My Defender, my Redeemer and Protector, You have given me the Holy Spirit as my Comforter and Guide.

I am no longer forsaken, and my spirit will no longer be grieved. You look upon me with great mercy and You gather me unto Yourself. With everlasting kindness, You have mercy on me. Your everlasting covenant keeps me, and Your promise of unfailing love is my portion. You have sworn that You will never rebuke me or be wrathful with me again, just as You promised Your servant Noah that the waters would never cover the earth again. The mountains may be removed, and the hills may shake, but Your kindness shall not depart from me, and Your covenant of peace shall never be removed.

Bind me up, Lord, and heal my wounds; according to Jeremiah 30:17, I am no longer an outcast, Your plans for me are good, plans of peace and not evil to give me a future and a hope. Your ears are inclined unto my prayers, and You hover over me with compassion. You soothe me with Your tender love because You have called me Your own.

I seek only Your kingdom. I return to my fortress. I am no longer a prisoner. You restore my life. You bring me up; You increase my honor and comfort me again.

Father, I take my compensation for the years the locust has eaten. I declare that I will eat in abundance and be satisfied; my household and I will praise the name of my God who is working wonders for me, and I will never again be ashamed.

When I am weak, You're strong. You provide for me, and my cup runs over. You prepare a place for me in the presence of my enemy, and my soul is quiet before you. You, O Lord are perfecting my faith. You endured the cross, despising its shame.

Take away the feelings of depression, anger, grief, pain, distress, unforgiveness and abandonment. Make me a fortified city; make me impenetrable by the evil one; cover me with the blood of Jesus; hide me under the shadow of Your wings.

Lay my foundations with sapphires, my windows of agates, my walls of crystals and my borders of precious stones. Beautify my life and give me beauty for ashes, the oil of joy for mourning, the garment of praise for the spirit of heaviness, that I may be called a tree of righteousness, planted and established by You Yourself.

You are near to the broken hearted. You're the strength of my heart. You're my portion forever. I will not let my heart be troubled because I know whose I am. You're with me wherever I go. All things are working together for my good according to Your purpose. I am delivered from the power of darkness and transformed into the kingdom of Your dear Son, and I have unlimited resources.

Today I declare and decree that I build the old ruins, I raise up the former desolation, I repair the waste cities, the desolations of many generations. Strangers shall stand and feed my flocks and the sons of aliens shall be my plowmen and vinedressers.

Enlarge my territory, O Lord. I will lengthen my cords and strengthen my stakes; I will spread out on the right hand and to the left, and my descendants will inherit the nations.

Oppression and terror are far from me. I will not fear. It is a righteous thing for God to trouble those who trouble me.

Whosesoever troubles me and assails me shall fall. You have struck the enemy down on my behalf and have muzzled the enemy at the gates. Deal with all my oppressors and change my shame into praise. I take refuge in You, for You are my stronghold in the day of trouble. I prevail in the power of Your might and no weapon formed against me shall prosper. Every lying tongue and judgment revolting against me is condemned and brought to nothing. For this is my heritage as a servant of the Lord and my vindication. You're not slow to fulfill Your promise. I will take no part in unfruitful work or idleness; I renounce disgraceful, underhanded ways. I am fruitful and productive. I abound in grace and my life is renewed, for out of me flows rivers of living water because I put my trust in You.

Instead of my shame I receive and take double honor; instead of humiliation I rejoice over my portion. In this land I possess a double portion, and everlasting joy shall be mine. I receive my sevenfold restoration and I decree today that I am delivered, healed, whole and restored in the mighty name of Jesus!

Blessed be the name of the Lord forever.

Scriptures

Grief: Psalm 34:18, Psalm 73:26, Psalm 147:3, Isiah 53:4–6, Joshua 1:9, Romans 1:9, Matthew 5:4, Revelation 21:4.

Shame: Isaiah 61:7, Isaiah 54:4, Revelation 21:4.

Forgiveness: Ephesians 4:32, Matthew 18:21–22, Matthew 6:14–15, Luke 17:3–4, 1 John 1:9, Isaiah 43:25–26, Colossians 1:13–14, Colossians 3:13, 2 Corinthians 5:17, Psalm 103:12, Mark 11:25.

Restoration: Joel 2:25–26, Jeremiah 30:17, Psalm 51:12, Amos 9:14, Exodus 21:34, Isaiah 61:7, Jeremiah 17:14, Job 42:10, 1 John 5:4, 1 Peter 5:10, John 14:1, Mark 11:24, Psalm 51:12, Zechariah 9:12, Psalm 71:20–21, 2 Corinthians 13:9–11, Psalm 23.

References

Nwanegbo, N.A. (1996): Challenge of Widowhood, Enugu, Sonnie
    Organization Ltd, pp. 11–13.

Nzewi, D. (1981): "Widowhood Practices: A Female Perspective," A
Paper Presented at a Workshop on Widowhood Practices in Imo
State, Nigeria, June 6–7.

WikiPedia. Nigerian civil war. Retreived September 29, 2018, from

https://en.wikipedia.org/wiki/Nigerian_Civil_War